Painting
with
Brenda Harris

GRUMBACHER

About the Artist

Brenda Harris was raised in a small North Carolina farming community. In college, while finishing her degree in business administration, Brenda took her first painting class—she was 31 at the time, and her world turned upside down. She took as many art classes as she could manage, and practiced to develop her own unique painting style. Her favored medium is acrylics, because of their versatility.

Brenda has been teaching on national television since 1987. Her enthusiasm, attention to detail and easy-to-master techniques have enabled thousands of students to be successful at acrylic painting. Brenda lives in Jacksonville, Florida, but spends much of her time traveling, teaching painting classes and workshops.

For more information, send a stamped, self-addressed envelope to Brenda Harris Seminars, P. O. Box 350155, Jacksonville, FL 32235-0155.

I dedicate this book to Koh-I-Noor. Because of their commitment to education, they have made this book possible. I am truly thankful.

Production Credits
Project editors: Sara Champion, Mary Margaret Hite
Photographers: Don Vallereux, Meredith Marsh
Graphic designer: Sally Clarke
Editors: Teresa Nelson, Tom Muir
Digital imagers: Shawn Jarvey, Michael Kincaid

Produced by  for  GRUMBACHER

M. Grumbacher, Inc.
A Koh-I-Noor Company
P.O. Box 68
Bloomington, NJ 08804-0068

1 2 3 4 5 6 7 8 9

Table of Contents

Koh-I-Noor Certified Artist Program

We hope you enjoy painting with Brenda Harris. For those of you who would like to work individually with an art educator, you may call the **Koh-I-Noor Certified Artists Program** to find an artist to work with in your area.

The **Koh-I-Noor Certified Artists Program** is a group of art educators throughout North America who offer classes for beginning, intermediate and advanced painters. All of the artists work with materials provided by Koh-I-Noor, the makers of Grumbacher, Rotring and Accent art materials.

Koh-I-Noor Certified Artists offer classes in a variety of mediums including acrylics, oils, and watercolor painting, as well as pencil and pen-and-ink drawing. For information on the **KCA** nearest you, please write KCA Program, P.O. Box 68, Bloomington, NJ 08804-0068.

Grumbacher Hotline

The folks at Grumbacher are pleased to help you with any questions you may have about materials. Call 1-800-FINE ART, Monday through Friday 8:30–4:30 EST.

Let's Paint with Acrylics!

Acrylics are a wonderful world of artistic expression. They are perfect for any age or level of expertise, providing both the beginner and the professional with a chance to explore unlimited avenues of creativity.

Versatility: Their versatility goes beyond traditional painting surfaces of canvas and paper. You can easily paint acrylics on wood, leather, glass, fabric, or any non-oily surface. With the addition of mediums, gels, modeling paste or varnishes, acrylics can open up other fields of art such as collage and assemblage.

Permanence: The acrylic polymer binders in these paints will remain flexible when dry. They do not oxidize, crack or peel.

Convenience: The paints dry the day you paint them. Paintings of great detail can be finished quickly—there's no need to wait to apply the finishing touches.

Value: You will find acrylic paints and mediums are less expensive in comparison to oil paints of the same quality. No high-priced solvents or thinners are needed. The brushes and tools also generally cost less than those for oil or watercolor. You need only water for mixing.

Materials

Paints

Grumbacher Acrylic Colors are the best acrylic formulation on the market, with the highest quality of pure pigments. They have superior adhesion and tinting strength. 72 colors are available in tubes, 48 colors in jars. Following is a list of the Grumbacher Acrylic tube colors used in this book:

Burnt Sienna

Burnt Umber

Cadmium Red Light

Cadmium Yellow Light

Cadmium Yellow Medium

Cerulean Blue

Chromium Oxide Green

Cobalt Titanate Green

Green Gold

Grumbacher Gray

Grumbacher Purple (Dioxazine Purple)

Grumbacher Red (Naphthol Red)

Hooker's Green

Iridescent White

Mars Black

Monoazo Orange

Portrayt™ (Red Oxide)

Prussian Blue

Raw Sienna

Raw Umber

Thalo® Crimson

Thalo® Gold

Thalo® Green

Thio™ Violet (Quinacridone Magenta)

Titanium White

Ultramarine Blue

Yellow Ochre Light

Mediums

Acrylic painting mediums are used in a number of ways to alter the brushing, textural and drying characteristics of the paint. Following is a list of the Grumbacher mediums used in this book, with their uses:

Whiteblend Acrylic Medium: This white pigment is excellent for creating soft, subtle colors with the exact amount of coverage required for the techniques covered in this text. The unique formula is formulated for proper consistency, slows drying time and allows you to blend colors easily. Whiteblend is the major ingredient for all of the paintings in this book. It is unlike any other paint on the market today. You must have it—there is no suitable substitute.

Clearblend Acrylic Medium: This adds transparency to your colors but does not change the value. It appears white when dispensed but dries clear. Clearblend dries at the same rate as Whiteblend and is permanent when dry. Apply Clearblend to an area before you begin painting, or streak it over wet paint with a clean, moist brush. Apply it on the edge of wet paint to create an even transition of color. Use it to create soft edges, transparent glazes and gradual blends and washes.

Slowblend Acrylic Medium: A clear liquid used to delay the drying time of acrylic paints, it will also add transparency. Mix with paints (use 3 parts paint to 1 part Slowblend) or apply directly to your canvas whenever you want to work colors together wet-on-wet. When layering applications of paint and Slowblend, you must wait longer between layers than with other mediums. Slowblend cures more slowly than other mediums and you may experience color lifting if you rush the process.

Grumbacher Acrylic Retarder: This is a thick, colorless medium that also slows the drying time of acrylic colors; it dries slightly faster than Slowblend. It is especially good when working wet-on-wet. It may be added to the paint up to 20% by volume.

Grumbacher Matte Medium/Varnish: Use to seal the edges of masking tape border. It dries to a clear, flat finish, and can also be used as a final varnish if you prefer to use a brush-on rather than an aerosol.

Grumbacher Modeling Paste: Create raised patterns and textures with this white texturizing medium. Apply thickly, using a plastic fork or other texturing tool to create patterns in the wet medium. Allow to dry overnight before painting over it. You can paint on top of the dried texture or mix colors into the medium before applying it to the canvas.

Grumbacher Acrylic Painting Varnish: This solvent-based spray final varnish is non-yellowing, quick drying, has a low gloss and can be removed with artists' solvents (turpentine or Pre-Tested Odorless Thinner). A few days after your painting is completed, spray it with this varnish to enhance the colors and protect them from dirt, dust, moisture, smoke and scuffs.

Brushes

Grumbacher brushes are second to none. These are the brushes you will need:

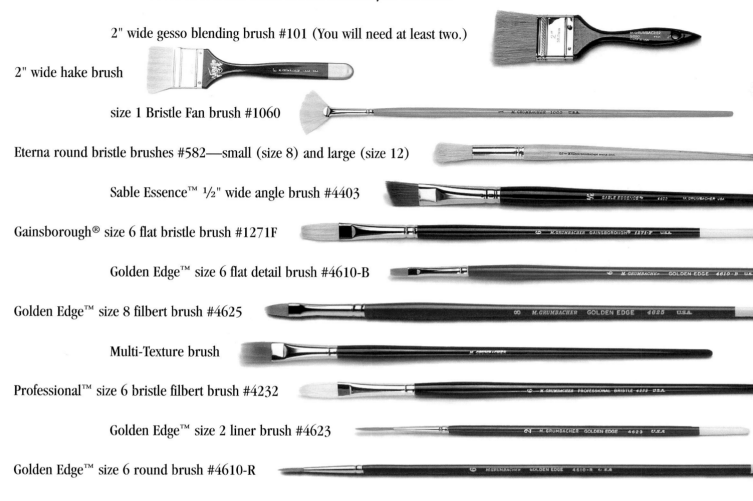

2" wide gesso blending brush #101 (You will need at least two.)

2" wide hake brush

size 1 Bristle Fan brush #1060

Eterna round bristle brushes #582—small (size 8) and large (size 12)

Sable Essence™ ½" wide angle brush #4403

Gainsborough® size 6 flat bristle brush #1271F

Golden Edge™ size 6 flat detail brush #4610-B

Golden Edge™ size 8 filbert brush #4625

Multi-Texture brush

Professional™ size 6 bristle filbert brush #4232

Golden Edge™ size 2 liner brush #4623

Golden Edge™ size 6 round brush #4610-R

Other Supplies

canvas: I prefer to use pre-stretched and primed canvas rather than to prepare one from scratch. All the paintings in this book require 16"x20" canvases.

Grumbacher Tapered Painting Knife #877-18

technical pens and ink. In this book I use four different sizes of **Koh-I-Noor Rapidograph** pens: .30, .35, .60 and 2.00. I use either Koh-I-Noor Rapidograph #3080R India Ink or Transparent Brown Rotring Artist Color.

natural sea wool sponge—Select a hand-sized sponge with as many "points" as possible.

white and charcoal graphite paper (for transferring the patterns)

Grumbacher Wet Palette (see page 8)

adhesive design protector sheets

Grumbacher Brush Soap

paper towels, kneaded artist's eraser, masking tape, stylus, pencil

Techniques

Grumbacher Wet Palette

This is a good way to keep acrylics wet on the palette for as long as you choose, letting you use paint that was mixed hours or even days before.

Saturate the sponge pad with as much water as it will hold. Spread it out in the plastic tray and add clean water until the pad almost floats. Soak a sheet of paper in clean water until completely wet. (The tray lid is ideal for this.) Place the paper on the pad. Use a damp sponge to remove puddles and smooth wrinkles.

Place your paints on the palette paper and begin mixing the desired colors. The paint will stay workable as long as the sponge pad remains wet. Keep the pad soggy at all times when the palette box is open. The pad dries out around the edges as the water evaporates, causing the paper to curl. When this happens, lift up the corner of the paper, pour water over the pad and press the paper back in place. If the paper has dried, moisten the top again. Place the lid on the tray when you need to store mixed paints.

Saturate the sponge pad.

Squeeze paints onto the wet paper.

Rewet the pad as necessary.

Mixing Colors

Along one side of your palette paper, dispense a marble-sized dollop of each tube pigment required.

Mixing colors, like painting, is an art—not a science! it is up to you to decide the exact hues. There are guidelines, but no exact formulas. Most color mixtures in this book are listed in order of the quantity used; some approximate proportions are given. It is easier to add color to a mixture than to subtract it, so always start with small portions.

Often it's best to mix colors directly on the brush or sponge. This is particularly useful when only a small amount is needed or when a gradual change of value or color is desired, as when highlighting an object.

All the projects in this book require some, but not all, colors to be prepared before you begin. This is particularly important for backgrounds, when a large amount is needed, or when working time for the application is limited. For these mixtures, use a clean painting knife to pull a small amount (about the size of a pea) of the first pigment listed from the dollop on the side of the palette. Add the other colors in lesser amounts and mix into a uniform shade. Adjust the color as needed; when a mixture is way off, avoid wasting paint by correcting only a part of it. When you have determined the right proportions, mix a larger amount that you think you'll need. Often more paint is required than you expect, and the excess is handy for touchups.

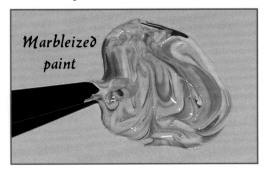

Marbleized paint

Unless the instructions state otherwise, paint mixtures should have the consistency of Whiteblend. Occasionally, the instructions will call for a *watery* consistency—add enough water to the paint to give it the density of ink. When instructed to create a *marbleized* mixture, do not blend the paints completely, but rather leave a mottled, streaky appearance.

Transferring and Protecting the Design

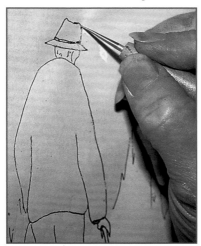

Transferring the pattern

Select the appropriate pattern from the pullout section of this book. Lay the canvas on a flat, sturdy surface. Refer to the painting instructions to position the pattern, then tape it firmly in place. Insert a piece of graphite paper between the pattern and canvas; trace the lines with a stylus or pencil to transfer them. Lift a corner of the graphite paper to see if you missed any lines.

When the directions require an adhesive design protector, use the same technique to trace only the outline onto the adhesive paper. Cut out the image, remove the backing and press it onto the canvas.

Paint carefully around the adhesive protector. Start with the brush on the cutout area and stroke away from it. If you stroke toward the cutout, you will force paint underneath it.

If transfer lines remain after the painting is finished, dry the area thoroughly and erase the lines with a kneaded eraser or clean moist sponge.

Applying adhesive protector

Removing the protector after painting

Drying your Painting

While watching the program, you may notice that I frequently use a hair dryer to speed up the drying process. Keep a hair dryer handy when you paint—it can save you a lot of time between steps. Hold the hair dryer a few inches away from the canvas. Do not set it on high heat or hold it in one position. Use a low temperature and move the dryer around the canvas.

Applying Paints

Familiarize yourself: Study the color placements of the painting. Read through the instructions, visualizing how you are going to execute each step. Have a piece of canvas or a scrap of watercolor paper handy to test your colors and strokes before applying them to the painting.

Working wet-on-wet is easy. Use a clean, towel-dried brush or sponge and work quickly.

Working wet-on-dry is easier. Use a clean, moist brush or tool. This technique allows you to work as quickly or as slowly as you desire.

Working wet-on-sticky is tricky! Add Clearblend or Slowblend to the sticky area of paint, allow the paint to dry thoroughly, then touch up with a wet-over-dry technique.

Removing excess water

Loading the brushes: Always moisten your brushes before using them. Before loading with paint, remove excess water from large brushes by squeezing the bristles. Tap smaller brushes on a clean towel. If the paint does not seem to be penetrating the pores of the canvas, moisten the brush again.

Double loading: This refers to applying two colors to the brush at one time. Painting with a double-loaded brush saves time and energy. It is easier to apply two colors at the same time, especially when creating delicate details such as birds or tree limbs.

Load the brush with the darkest color of the subject matter. Pull one side of the brush through the highlight color to create a dark and a light side. Position the brush so the stroke will be half dark and half light as you touch the canvas.

Double loading

Loading the knife

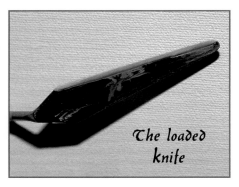

The loaded knife

Loading a painting knife: Use the knife to spread the paint in a thin layer across the palette. Remove the paint from the knife. Hold the knife edge in the paint and pull back diagonally to load a ribbon of paint along the edge.

Blending colors: Apply each color quickly and generously, overlapping them at least ½". Use a clean, towel-dried brush and work over the overlapped area with elongated figure-8 strokes, frequently wiping the excess paint off the brush. When the colors are mingled, blend with long strokes, brushing back and forth and moving from light colors into dark ones. Begin blending with firm pressure; use a feather touch for the finishing strokes. A hake brush is good for the finishing touches.

Pat-blending: Load a bristle brush generously with Clearblend, lightly wiping off excess on a paper towel. Apply the highlight color with the corner of a fan brush, then pat with the bristle brush to soften the edges into the background color. Don't work too hard to blend the colors smoothly—an irregular look is more natural.

Highlights, shadows and catchlights: Blend lighter color into a highlighted area, darker colors into areas which are shaded. On a smooth, polished surface (such as a bubble or an eye) a highlight has a sharper edge and is called a catchlight. These may simply be dots of a brighter color.

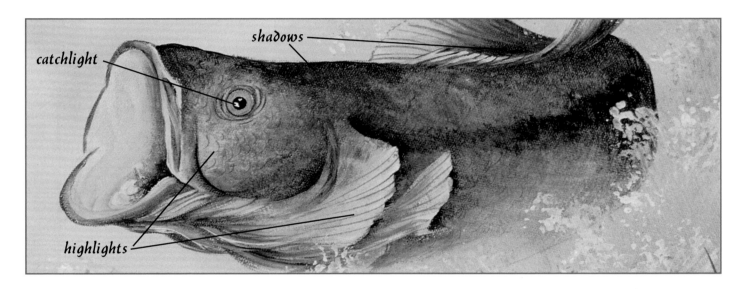

C-strokes

C-strokes: C-strokes are used to create the bottoms of waves, feathers, and the scales on a fish. Use a short, curving stroke to pull the wet paint into an elongated "C" shape.

Crunching a Color

Crunching, stippling and tapping: Occasionally the instructions call for you to "crunch" in a color. Hold the loaded brush perpendicular to the canvas and push straight in, fanning the bristles out a bit. "Stippling" uses the same motion with a little less pressure; "tapping" uses even less pressure than stippling.

Contrast, perspective and depth:
Place dark colors against light and light colors against dark. Darker, more vibrant colors are generally placed in the foreground; lighter, muted colors are applied in the background. Objects of medium value are placed in between.

The more distant the object is, the smaller it becomes and the closer it appears to the horizon line. The middle ground objects will be lower on the canvas, larger, and more defined. The foreground objects are lowest on the canvas, largest in size and most sharply focused.

Brighter objects move forward.

Objects on the horizon are lighter and smaller.

Drying time: Acrylics dry at an uneven rate. Often the outer edges of an application begin to dry first. This can cause a spotty appearance when drying, but the color will even out when it is completely dry. Acrylics will be darker when dry than while wet.

Two techniques that will extend a painting's dry time: Moisten the canvas with water before applying paint, or add a few drops of Slowblend or Grumbacher Acrylic Retarder to each tube color on your palette before mixing. Do not add more than ⅓ medium to ⅔ paint.

Signing your painting: Stand back and look over your painting. Believe it or not, it will be even more beautiful tomorrow! You can sign your painting with watery acrylic paint or a Koh-I-Noor Rapidograph pen.

Cleaning your brushes: Wash your brushes with Grumbacher Brush Soap. The lid of the soap container has a "ridged" cleaning surface. Lather the brush and lightly scrub it on the grid. Rinse; towel dry. This will clean and condition the brushes at the same time. Allow them to dry flat to avoid bent bristles. Rinse out the lid of the container and replace it on the cleaner.

Dry acrylic paint can be removed from brushes or other areas with alcohol. Denatured alcohol from the hardware store works best. If a brush is hard with acrylic paint, you may need to soak it for a few minutes before attempting to remove the paint. Be careful with the alcohol—it can remove the finish from some furniture!

Special Techniques

Throughout this book I use a wide variety of techniques for creating foliage, skies and water. Duplicating techniques demonstrated by others accelerates and broadens your ability to be independently creative. Try mixing and matching these techniques in your own compositions.

Skies are supposed to be streaky.

Skies: Work quickly, blocking in the sky colors with a generous amount of paint. Overlap colors ½" or more. Blend immediately with a clean, towel-dried brush until the desired effect is achieved.

Half-dry skies always look streaked, and you might have the urge to go back and overwork it: don't. Allow it to dry completely. After the painting is finished, you will find that a streak or two in the background or sky is realistic. If you absolutely cannot accept your sky after it is dry, touch it up with a wet-on-dry technique or paint over it as though you were painting on a clean, new surface.

Reflections and water lines: Water works like a mirror, picking up images and colors around it. Visualize your subject matter sitting on a mirror and paint the reflection accordingly. Keep all predominant strokes horizontal. Reflections can be painted wet-on-wet or added to a dry surface.

Add horizontal water lines to make the reflections appear to be underwater. Load the painting knife with Whiteblend and place the edge against the canvas. Soften the edges with a clean brush moistened with Clearblend. For more coverage, hold the knife at a 45° angle. To paint a tide line, gradually turn the knife even flatter on the canvas as you move it across.

Reflections

Making waves

Ocean waves: Oceans and waves can be painted either wet-on-wet or wet-on-dry. Apply the basic colors and blend using wet-on-wet technique.

For distant whitecaps, add a horizontal highlight with either a painting knife or a liner brush. Soften or blend the bottom and side edges with a brush moistened with Clearblend.

Sponge on a group of bushes.

Foliage: Foliage and foliage highlights can be painted with brushes or sponges, applied wet-on-wet or wet-on-dry. To create foliage with a sponge, load a small section with paint and tap irregular leaves on the canvas.

The most widely used brushes for stippling foliage are bristle brushes. The foliage can be dense or sparse, depending on the pressure of application. To create sparse foliage, use light pressure. For dense foliage, use light pressure on the edges but heavier pressure in the center. You can also use a brush or painting knife to fill in the center. While the paint is still wet, pat over it with a moist sponge to texture it.

Sponge again for shadows and highlights.

Apply highlights sparsely and use light pressure throughout. To achieve a rounded appearance, tap the canvas lightly. Use less of the color and a lighter touch when applying each highlight; never block out all the base foliage color.

Apply the darkest or dullest highlight ¾ of the way around the foliage. Add the middle-value highlight more sparingly, about halfway around the foliage. The brightest highlight is lightly stippled on the front ¼. Any reflected lights are sparingly applied to the darkest, shadowy areas of the foliage.

Stipple the brightest highlights in front.

Press firmly to flare bristles.

Grass: When creating a thick field of grass wet-on-wet, use large gesso brushes. Alternate one brush loaded with light color and another loaded with dark. Holding the brush perpendicular to the canvas, press firmly until the bristles begin to flare out. Hold the pressure firmly and crunch with a slightly upward thrust. Do not allow the bristles to slide upward. Done properly, the brush bristles will arch slightly and the top outer bristles will flare out, creating many irregular lengths of grass blades. Use several colors and values of colors from your composition.

To avoid bare spots, each additional row should flare up slightly over the base of the previous one. Begin with a light color in the distance and end with a dark color at the bottom of the canvas. Add a contrasting patch of color in one area to create additional depth.

An easy way to create field grass wet-on-dry is to base coat the grass areas with the appropriate colors for your composition. The darkest color should be at the bottom of the canvas. Stipple accent and highlight colors over the dry base coat.

Start accenting the grass with the least contrasting accent color that will be in that area. A fan brush is most convenient in the distant fields and for final detail in the foreground. Use the large gesso brush for the least contrasting colors in the foreground.

Add final detail with a fan brush.

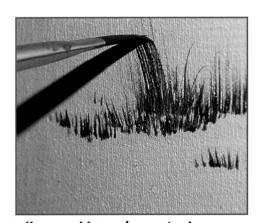

Pull grass blades from the bottom up.

Use a Multi-Texture or fan brush for clusters of grass or marsh grass. Hold the brush perpendicular to the canvas and apply watery paint from the root up. Lift up taller grasses with a liner brush.

The Multi-Texture is the best brush for painting marsh grasses. Work the paint wet-on-wet. Alternating and overlapping the light and dark paint will create a variety of colors and values. All water lines must be flat, so keep rows of marsh grass parallel to the bottom of the canvas. Cover the water area below the grass with Clearblend and paint a reflection (see page 14).

Use a liner for individual tall blades.

Correcting Mistakes

Are you afraid of making a mistake while painting? Don't be! Know up front that you will make a mistake occasionally. We all do. No matter how long you paint or how masterful you become as an artist, you will make a mistake from time to time. The only people not making mistakes are those people who are doing nothing at all.

Anything you put on your canvas can be corrected. If it is wet, you simply wipe it off. If dry, you can scrub it off with a toothbrush moistened with Slowblend. For tougher jobs, use a wire brush from the hardware store, or simply paint over it!

Because acrylics dry quickly, it is best to stop and fix obvious errors as they occur. Keep a clean, damp sponge handy to wipe them out. It is also best to dry your painting thoroughly between steps; then errors will simply wipe off, leaving the dry paint undisturbed.

If you have painted a "fat" limb or a crooked line, you know it right away. Use a clean, moist angle brush to push excess paint back into the line or remove it.

If you have really goofed—and the goofy thing has dried—you can still fix the painting. If it is a mistake covering a large area, just paint over it. Train yourself to think creatively! Could you cover it with foliage or a cloud?

The best source of correcting techniques can be viewed as they are demonstrated in my workshops. Hope to see you there!

Now, let's paint!

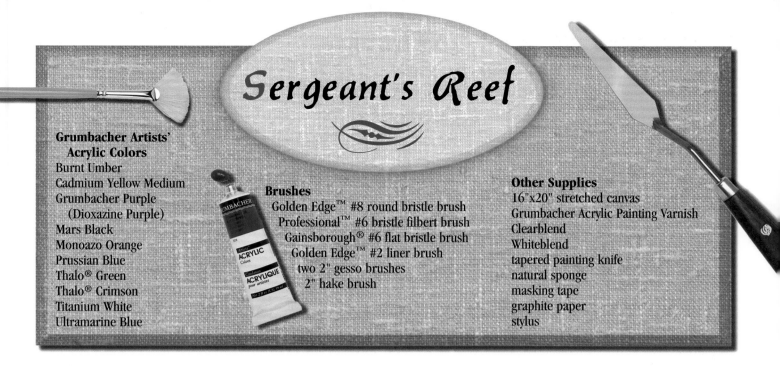

Sergeant's Reef

Grumbacher Artists'
Acrylic Colors
Burnt Umber
Cadmium Yellow Medium
Grumbacher Purple
   (Dioxazine Purple)
Mars Black
Monoazo Orange
Prussian Blue
Thalo® Green
Thalo® Crimson
Titanium White
Ultramarine Blue

Brushes
Golden Edge™ #8 round bristle brush
Professional™ #6 bristle filbert brush
Gainsborough® #6 flat bristle brush
Golden Edge™ #2 liner brush
   two 2" gesso brushes
      2" hake brush

Other Supplies
16"x20" stretched canvas
Grumbacher Acrylic Painting Varnish
Clearblend
Whiteblend
tapered painting knife
natural sponge
masking tape
graphite paper
stylus

Note: Throughout this book, look for large "painting-in-progress" shots like the one below, interspersed with smaller shots illustrating specific techniques.

Palette
Before you begin, prepare these color mixtures.
sea green—Whiteblend, Thalo® Green, Cadmium Yellow Medium
dark blue—Prussian Blue, Grumbacher Purple; touch of Whiteblend
pink—Thalo® Crimson, Whiteblend
aquamarine—Prussian Blue, Thalo® Green, Whiteblend
pale blue—Ultramarine Blue, Whiteblend
bright yellow—Cadmium Yellow Medium, Titanium White

1 **Background:** Use a gesso brush to base coat the canvas *sea green*; dry thoroughly. Continue with the same brush to scrub the top two-thirds of the canvas with *Clearblend*.

2 While the *Clearblend* is still wet, paint more *sea green* in the canvas center. With the uncleaned brush, add *aquamarine, dark blue* and *pale blue* to the top and sides of the canvas, framing the light center. Blend with a clean, towel-dried gesso brush; use the hake brush for final blending. Do not blend the colors completely, but to give the illusion of light fading into dark.

3 Coral reef: Load your uncleaned brush with a mixture of *dark blue* and *pale blue,* creating a middle value. Holding the brush vertically, tap in an irregularly-shaped distant coral reef that is off-center to the left, but frames the light area in the center of the canvas.

4 Squeeze pure pigments right out of the tubes randomly around the bottom of the canvas. Apply *Grumbacher Purple* closest to the bottom of the distant coral reef, *Prussian Blue, Thalo® Green* and *Burnt Umber* on the bottom corners. Use a gesso brush to spread the colors, painting the canvas solidly below the distant coral reef.

5 Refer to the finished painting for the colors, shapes and locations of the coral spikes protruding from the reef. Create each section of spikes with a different color (either *Grumbacher Purple, Thalo® Crimson, Monoazo Orange* or *Thalo® Green*) as follows: Load a clean sponge or flat bristle brush with the pure tube color and create the basic shape of a section of spikes.

6 Mix *Whiteblend* into the color in the uncleaned sponge or brush and apply a variety of values of that color onto these spikes. Mix *Titanium White* (and more tube color, if needed) into the color in your uncleaned sponge or brush and sparingly add bright highlights to these spikes.

7 Clean the sponge or brush. Load it with another of the colors from step 5 and create another section of spikes. Repeat until all the spikes are painted.

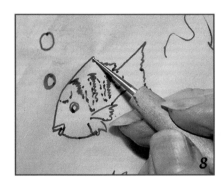

8 Sergeant Majors: When the canvas is completely dry, use white graphite paper to transfer the fish and bubbles into the dark areas between coral spikes on the reef.

9 With the round bristle brush, apply *Clearblend* inside the lines of each fish. Use the liner brush to paint *pale blue* around the outer edges of the fish. Use the filbert brush moistened with *Clearblend* to blend the inner edges of the *pale blue,* creating a gradual transition of color and leaving the center of the fish translucent.

10 While the bodies are still wet, add *pink* on the undersides of the bellies for reflected light. Use the filbert brush moistened with *Clearblend* to blend the upper edges of the pink. Dry thoroughly. Paint a line of *Whiteblend* down the center of the fish facing you. Moisten the filbert brush with *Clearblend* and gently blend each side of the line.

11 Use a mixture of *pale blue* and *Clearblend* for the translucent fins. Fill in the tails of the Sergeant Majors with *pale blue*. Dry. Use the liner brush with a mixture of *Whiteblend* and a touch of *pale blue*, thinned to the consistency of thick cream, to add the spines in the fins.

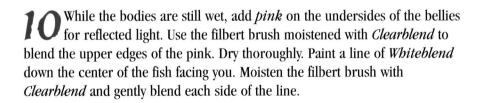

12 Paint the *bright yellow* and *Mars Black* stripes with the liner brush. Allow each stripe to dry completely before applying the next. Paint the eyes and eye rings *Mars Black*.

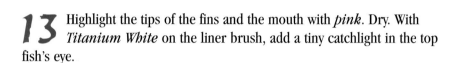

13 Highlight the tips of the fins and the mouth with *pink*. Dry. With *Titanium White* on the liner brush, add a tiny catchlight in the top fish's eye.

14 **Bubbles:** Each bubble gets larger as it floats upward. Use the liner brush to paint *pale blue* on the bubble bottoms. With the filbert or liner moistened with *Clearblend*, blend the inner edges of each bubble, leaving the center translucent. Let dry, then apply *Whiteblend* to the top and left sides, fading to the inside. Dry; add a catchlight to each bubble at 1:00.

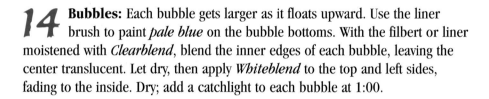

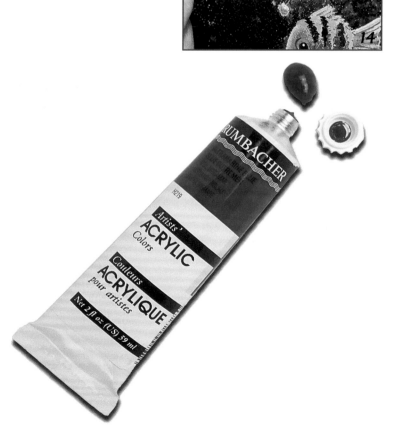

15 **Minnows:** Create your own formation for the minnows as you trace them onto the canvas. Place some distant fish randomly throughout the light center of the canvas. Fill the bodies with *dark blue*. Dry. Add reflected light by applying *pink* to the underside of each fish. Use the liner moistened with *Clearblend* to blend the upper edges of the pink.

16 Use a liner brush with *pink* to dot an eye on each fish. Dry the canvas.

17 Use watery *dark blue* on a liner brush to paint the distant twigs in the distant coral reef—pull the loaded liner upward from the coral, allowing the tips to taper and fade out. To "plant" the twigs in the coral, blot the still-wet bottom of each with your finger. Repeat for the foreground twigs, using a watery mixture of *dark blue* and *Burnt Umber* double loaded with *pink*.

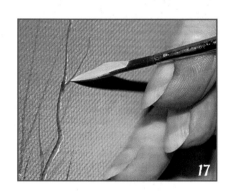

18 Once the canvas is dry, add more colors or highlights to the reef with a clean sponge as described in step 6. To correct any coral that is too large or too bright, use the sponge to dab on *dark blue* or the base color for that section of spikes.

Sign your painting with contrasting colors. Take a break and go diving with some friendly Sergeant Majors! When it's completely dry, spray your painting with Grumbacher Acrylic Painting Varnish.

Coming Home

Grumbacher Artists' Acrylic Colors
Burnt Sienna
Burnt Umber
Grumbacher Purple
  (Dioxazine Purple)
Hooker's Green
Mars Black
Monoazo Orange
Raw Sienna
Thio™ Violet (Quinacridone Magenta)
Ultramarine Blue
Yellow Ochre Light

Brushes
Sable Essence™ ½" angle brush
Golden Edge™ #8 filbert brush
Golden Edge™ #2 liner brush
Eterna #8 round bristle brush
two 2" gesso brushes
#1 Bristle Fan brush
Multi-Texture brush
2" hake brush

Other Supplies
16"x20" stretched canvas
Grumbacher Acrylic Painting Varnish
Clearblend
Whiteblend
Slowblend
tapered painting knife
natural sponge
masking tape
graphite paper, stylus

Palette
Before you begin, prepare these color mixtures.
gray— Ultramarine Blue, Burnt Sienna, Whiteblend
off-white—Whiteblend, Yellow Ochre Light; touch of
  Monoazo Orange
wheat—Yellow Ochre Light, Whiteblend
smoke—Burnt Umber, Mars Black, Whiteblend
light violet-gray—Ultramarine Blue, Grumbacher Purple,
  Burnt Umber
dark green—Burnt Umber, Thio™ Violet, Hooker's Green
salmon—Whiteblend, Monoazo Orange, Yellow Ochre
  Light

Prepare these color mixtures as you need them.
medium brown—Burnt Umber, Burnt Sienna, Whiteblend
dark brown—medium brown, Burnt Umber, touch of
  Grumbacher Purple
medium violet-gray—Ultramarine Blue, Grumbacher
  Purple, Burnt Umber
light sienna—Raw Sienna, Whiteblend, Slowblend
transparent glaze—watery Burnt Sienna, Slowblend

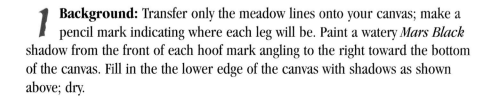

1 **Background:** Transfer only the meadow lines onto your canvas; make a
pencil mark indicating where each leg will be. Paint a watery *Mars Black*
shadow from the front of each hoof mark angling to the right toward the bottom
of the canvas. Fill in the the lower edge of the canvas with shadows as shown
above; dry.

2 **Sky:** Beginning at the horizon line, use a gesso brush to cover the bottom ¾ of the sky with *off-white*. Moving diagonally from the top left to the bottom right, add irregular diagonal *gray* streaks in the center of the sky. Moving diagonally from bottom right to top left, apply *off-white* streaks through the *gray* at the top. Towel-clean the brush and use it for the preliminary blending. Create the soft, blustery transition between the colors with the hake brush, using a dusting motion. Clean your blending brush frequently on paper towels during the blending process to create clean, smooth blends.

3 Load the round bristle brush with *Clearblend* and *gray*; stipple a lacy line of distant trees across the horizon. If the tree line is too solid, sparingly stipple *off-white* into the solid areas to create separations between trees.

4 **Meadow:** Use the fan brush to paint the distant meadow *wheat*. Add streaks of *smoke* along the lower edge and up into the wet meadow. Blend slightly.

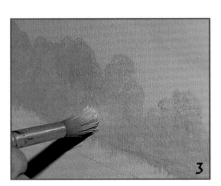

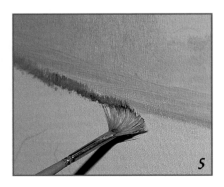

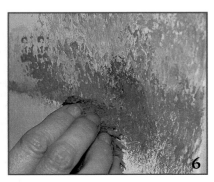

5 While the distant meadow is wet, brush-mix a touch of *Burnt Sienna* into the uncleaned brush and tap in a muted fence row of foliage across the canvas, connecting to the bottom of the distant meadow.

6 **Middle trees:** Load the moist sponge with *light violet-gray* and tap in the tallest middle foliage. Add *medium violet-gray* to the sponge for the lower bushes. For the darkest bushes, sponge-mix muted earth tones by alternately adding *Burnt Sienna* and *light violet gray*, *Monoazo Orange* and *light violet gray*, and *smoke* to the uncleaned sponge.

7 Use *wheat* on the fan brush to tap short grasses along the bottom of the middle foliage and fence row. Alternately apply *wheat* and the foliage colors to create a door-stepped progression in the middle foliage on the right of the canvas. Use a gesso brush to quickly paint the remaining foreground meadow *wheat*. While the meadow is still wet, create color variations through it by alternately brush-mixing *smoke, Burnt Sienna, Burnt Umber* and *dark green* into the *wheat*. Make the colors darker as you move toward the bottom of the canvas. Tap and blend these in the wet grass. Use a gesso brush with *dark green, Burnt Sienna* and *Burnt Umber* to stipple grasses over the *Mars Black* at the bottom of the canvas. While this is still wet, pat to blend with a clean fan brush, creating a gradual transition with light and dark areas of drifting light.

8 **Tree trunks:** Double load the angle brush with *smoke* and *salmon* so when the brush is positioned vertically *salmon* is on the left. Pull down from the top of the canvas, using very little pressure on the brush at the top of the tree. Gradually apply more pressure as you move downward, widening the tree trunk. Blot the bottoms of the trunks to "plant" them into the foliage.

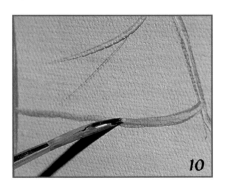

9 While the tree trunks are still wet, create the appearance of bark by patting the *salmon* highlight randomly to soften the transition. Add the final detail after the trunks are dry by first moistening the trunks with *Clearblend,* then adding the additional bark highlights or shadows. Dry.

10 Apply the tree limbs with a liner brush and a watery mixture of *salmon* and *Slowblend*. Use very light pressure on the brush, releasing the pressure as you paint to taper the limb tips. Use a clean moist sponge to wipe off any mistakes while they are still wet. When the first limbs are dry, double load *smoke* and *salmon* to make a few additional limbs.

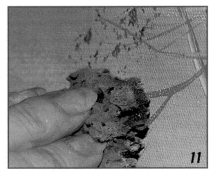

11 Use the moist sponge with a mixture of earth tones (corresponding to the colors of the foliage beneath the trees) to apply sparse leaves on the trees. If needed, tap in more low foliage around the bases of the tree trunks with the same paints. Dry.

12 **Deer:** Use a watery liner brush and *Mars Black* to paint his muzzle, eyes and ear markings. Dry. Use the angle and filbert brushes with *medium brown* to base coat the deer. As you apply the base coat, also shade the neck, ears and inner legs with *dark brown*, wet-on-wet.

13 Look at the finished painting for highlight placement. Brush *Clearblend* over the deer. While it is still wet, use the angle brush to cover him with a watery *Burnt Sienna* glaze. While the *Clearblend* and glaze are still wet, apply *Raw Sienna* highlights over the top of his back, neck and all other sunlit areas of his body. Fade the highlight downward into the *Clearblend*. Dry.

14 For the final highlights, apply and blend one sunlit spot at a time. With your angle brush, apply a *light sienna* highlight over the top of the deer's back and neck. Moisten the Multi-Texture brush with *Clearblend* and fade the lower edges of the highlight. Hold your brush perpendicular to the canvas and pat to blend, using very light pressure.

15 With the liner or Multi-Texture brush, apply *medium violet-gray* shadow markings to the legs, neck, tail, ears and underbelly. Dry. Add a touch of *off-white* to the brush and highlight the *violet*. Smudge *off-white* around the eyes and muzzle. Add a *medium brown* iris inside the eye socket. Touch up the pupil with *Mars Black* and add a *Whiteblend* catchlight at 2:00.

16 Double load the liner brush with *dark brown* and *light sienna*, then paint the antlers. Dry.

17 **Foreground:** Add the foreground foliage with a gesso brush. Load the brush with *Grumbacher Purple*, push it into the bottom of the canvas, and paint with an upward stroke. Use the same technique to apply *Raw Sienna*, *Burnt Sienna*, *Monoazo Orange* and *dark green*.

18 While the foreground is still wet, blot with a clean moist sponge, creating texture. Use the fan brush with the same colors to add tall grasses for detail.

19 Add *wheat* and *light sienna* to the liner brush and paint individual grass blades in the foreground. With the corner of your fan brush, tap in *Ultramarine Blue* and *Monoazo Orange* flowers.

20 When the canvas is dry, use the liner brush to add a small watery *dark brown* tree on the left side. Use the liner brush with watery *dark brown* to paint the branches; highlight with *light violet-gray*. Mix a watery *dark brown* to paint the dead trees and twigs.

21 Double load the liner brush with *smoke* and *salmon* to paint the fence posts. Paint the wires watery *light violet-gray*.

Sign and head for home! Spray with Grumbacher Acrylic Painting Varnish when completely dry.

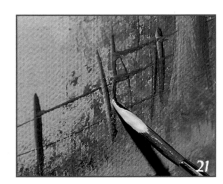

Twilight Flight

Grumbacher Artists' Acrylic Colors
Burnt Umber
Burnt Sienna
Cadmium Yellow Medium
Grumbacher Purple
   (Dioxazine Purple)
Mars Black
Monoazo Orange
Yellow Ochre Light

Brushes
Sable Essence™ ½" angle brush
Golden Edge™ #8 filbert brush
Golden Edge™ #2 liner brush
Multi-Texture brush
#1 Bristle Fan brush
two 2" gesso brushes
2" hake brush

Other Supplies
16"x20" stretched canvas
Grumbacher Acrylic Painting Varnish
Whiteblend
Clearblend
Slowblend
tapered painting knife
natural sponge
masking tape, graphite paper, stylus

Palette
Before you begin, prepare these color mixtures.
dusty peach—1 part Whiteblend, 2 parts Monoazo
   Orange, 2 parts Burnt Umber, 1 part Cadmium
   Yellow Medium
medium yellow—Whiteblend, Yellow Ochre Light
dark brown—4 parts Burnt Umber, 2 parts Burnt
   Sienna, 1 part Grumbacher Purple, 2 parts
   Slowblend
mauve—Whiteblend, dusty peach, dark brown

Prepare these color mixtures as you need them.
bright yellow—Whiteblend, Cadmium Yellow Medium
black—2 parts Grumbacher Purple, 2 parts Mars
   Black, 1 part Slowblend
violet-gray—black, Whiteblend

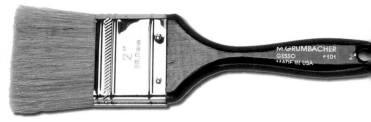

1 **Background:** Use a gesso brush to base coat the canvas *dusty peach*. Dry
thoroughly. Transfer the water lines and the background tree line, placing
them so the most distant water line is 3¾" above the bottom of the canvas.(You
will transfer the goose after you paint the foliage.) Dampen the canvas with
clean water, then brush *Clearblend* over the wet sky area. While the area is still
wet, use a gesso brush to apply *medium yellow* across the center of the sky
and extending downward to just below the top of the tree line. Blend slightly
toward the top of the canvas.

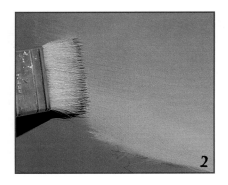

2 Add *dusty peach* to the uncleaned brush as you move toward the top of the sky. Blend with a clean gesso brush. Do the final blending with a hake brush.

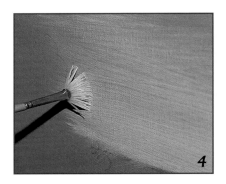

3 While the sky is wet, pat along the top of the tree line with a clean, moist sponge to blot off the *medium yellow,* leaving the shapes of the tree tops.

4 **Water**: To create mist above the water line, work the paint wet on wet. Use a clean gesso brush with *Clearblend* to moisten the tree area. Using the fan brush, apply *medium yellow* above the water toward the center of the canvas. Blend by brushing horizontally, slowly moving upward to create a gradual transition of color. Concentrate most of the color in the center of the canvas and gently fade it into the trees on the right. Load the sponge with *mauve* and pat along the top of the distant tree line to create the tree tops. Blend the bottom of the *mauve* into the wet *Clearblend.* Dry.

5 Use *Clearblend* to moisten the water area below the distant trees. Use the gesso brush or sponge to tap in a faint *mauve* reflection below the water line along the right side of the canvas. Blend and dry.

6 Apply *bright yellow* water lines with the painting knife. Hold the knife horizontally and tap it against the canvas. Dry.

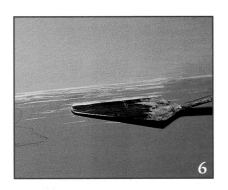

7 Sponge in the middle foliage with *mauve*. Darken the tree color gradually by adding more *dusty peach* and *dark brown* to your uncleaned sponge as you create denser foliage— hold a paper towel over the water line to create an edge. Dry. Add a touch of *dusty peach* to the sponge and tap a few highlights over the foliage.

8 Dampen the water with a gesso brush and *Clearblend*. Using horizontal strokes, apply *medium yellow* in the center of the wet water area. Streak *dusty peach* across the bottom of the canvas. To create the reflection, use a fan brush with *mauve, dusty peach* and *dark brown* to stroke downward under the foliage on on the left side of the canvas. Use *mauve* to strengthen the reflections on the right of the canvas if necessary. Create a zig-zag shimmer by brushing horizontally throughout the wet water area with a clean dry fan brush. Clean your blending brush frequently. Dry. Use the painting knife to apply *bright yellow* water lines. Increase the intensity of the water lines in the canvas center by adding *Whiteblend* to the *bright yellow*. Decrease the intensity of the waterlines in the shadow areas by adding *dusty peach* to the *bright yellow*.

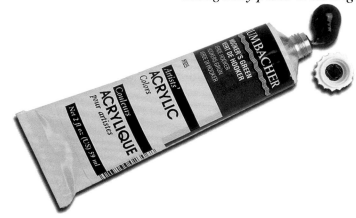

9 Apply *Clearblend* over the water under the foreground foliage. Using watery *dark brown* as the base color and the fan or Multi-Texture brush, add small islands of foreground grasses below the foliage. While the grass is still wet, gently pull down into the water to make a reflection. Add *dusty peach* to the uncleaned brush and streak dull highlights into the grass.

10 Add *Whiteblend* to the uncleaned fan or Multi-Texture brush and add brighter highlights to the grass. Dry. Add water lines to separate the grass from the reflections. Dry thoroughly.

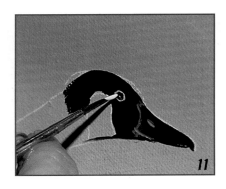

11 **Goose:** *(Note: Before applying dark colors to the goose, blend with water to the same consistency as Whiteblend. To soften unwanted hard lines or sharp edges, blot them with your finger or blend with a brush moistened with Clearblend.)* Use white graphite paper to transfer the goose so the eye is 3" from the top and 4" from the right edge of the canvas. Base coat the eye *black*. Dry, then use the liner brush to dot a *Whiteblend* catchlight in his eye, positioned about 1:00. Base coat the beak, head and neck *black*—to avoid "losing" the eye and beak, leave hairline unpainted outlines. Dry. Use the liner with watery *violet-gray* to add details on the beak and paint the eye ring. Dry.

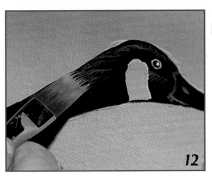

12 With the Multi-Texture brush and watery *violet-gray*, indicate tiny feather shapes on the head and neck. Paint the facial marking *violet-gray* on the bottom and *Whiteblend* on the cheek. While it's still wet, add a hint of *peach* reflected light to the marking and blend. Dry.

13 With the angle brush and *dark brown*, base coat the underside of the wing behind the body. Dry.

14 Use the liner brush and watery *violet-gray* to indicate reflected light on the feathers underneath the wing and the lines separating the primary and secondary feathers.

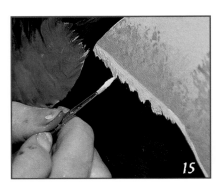

15 Paint the top of his left wing *bright yellow*, using the liner brush to make the edge ragged. Add *dusty peach* to highlight the edge. With the uncleaned brush, add a few *violet-gray* feather marks at the base of the neck.

16 Use the angle and Multi-Texture brushes with *dark brown* and the foreground tree colors to basecoat the back and body. While they are still wet, pat to blend the colors. Dry. Using the filbert brush and a C-stroke, paint *dusty peach* chest feathers. Concentrate the brightest of the feathers in the center of the chest, blending outward. While the feathers are still wet, add a touch of *Whiteblend* to your brush. Use a C-stroke to highlight the feathers in the center of the chest. Blend slightly, leaving the feather marks distinct. Add a touch of *violet-gray* to the brush and highlight the shadow of the chest.

17 Base coat the foreground wing in three overlapping sections which graduate in value from dark at the wing tip to light at the shoulder. Use the angle brush with *dark brown* for the primary feathers, *Burnt Umber* for the secondary feathers and center section, and *dusty peach* shaded with *dark brown* for the top or shoulder section. Dry. Base coat the tail and three "flipped-up" primary feathers on the closest wing with *black.* Dry thoroughly. If necessary, place the pattern over the goose and transfer the feather markings as a guide to add the details. With the liner brush and watery *violet-gray,* add reflected light on the edges of the tail and primary feathers.

18 Use a watery mixture of *medium yellow* and *dusty peach* with the liner and Multi-Texture brushes to add small feather detail marks on the top or shoulder section of the wing. Add *dusty peach* details to the middle wing section. Use watery *violet-gray* and the Multi-Texture brush to create feather marks on the large feathers. In the same way, add a few brighter marks with watery *dusty peach* on the feathers near the top of the wing.

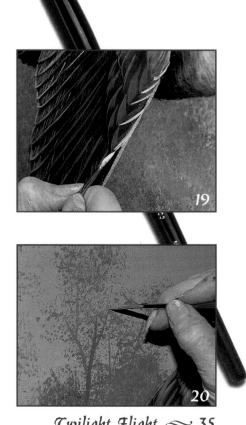

19 Add more watery *bright yellow* to your liner brush and paint the leading edges of the feathers on both wings.

20 With the liner brush loaded with *mauve,* add trunks and limbs to the distant trees.

Sign your painting. When it's thoroughly dry, finish with Grumbacher Acrylic Painting Varnish and move on!

Remember When

Grumbacher Artists' Acrylic Colors
Titanium White
Burnt Sienna
Cadmium Yellow Medium
Green Gold
Mars Black
Monoazo Orange
Ultramarine Blue

Brushes
Golden Edge™ #6 flat detail brush
Sable Essence™ ½" angle brush
Eterna #8 round bristle brush
Golden Edge™ #2 liner brush
two 2" gesso brushes
#1 Bristle Fan brush
2" hake brush

Other Supplies
16"x20" stretched canvas
Grumbacher Acrylic Painting Varnish
Clearblend
Whiteblend
Koh-I-Noor Rapidograph technical pen
  #0.60
tapered painting knife
adhesive design protector
masking tape
graphite paper, stylus

Palette
Before you begin, prepare these color mixtures.
peach—Whiteblend, Monoazo Orange
pale blue—Whiteblend, Ultramarine Blue
dark gray—10 parts Ultramarine Blue, 1 part
  Monoazo Orange
light violet-gray—Whiteblend, touch of dark gray
dark green—5 parts Ultramarine Blue, 2 parts
  Cadmium Yellow Medium, 1 part Mars Black
light gray-green—light violet-gray, touch of dark green
pastel gray-green—light gray-green, touch of dark
  green
medium green—pastel gray-green, dark green

Prepare these color mixtures as you need them.
pale yellow—Whiteblend, Cadmium Yellow Medium
sunny yellow—pale yellow, Cadmium Yellow Medium
off-white—Whiteblend, touch of pale yellow

1 **Background:** Use charcoal graphite paper to transfer the design to the
canvas, placing the tallest peak of the roof 6" from the top and 8" from the
right side. Go over the lines of the gas station with the pen. After the ink is dry,
place a design protector over the building. Use a gesso brush with *Mars Black*
to paint the foreground; dry.

2

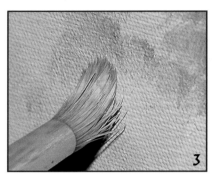

3

4

5

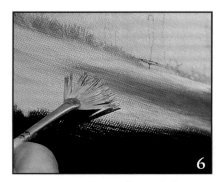

6

2 Using a clean gesso brush with *Whiteblend*, cover the sky area down to the top of the meadow. While the sky is still wet, add a touch of *peach* to the uncleaned brush and apply to the lower sky. Add *pale blue* to the brush and apply to the top of the sky. Blend with a clean, towel-dried gesso brush, eliminating bold streaks of color. Do the final blending with the hake brush.

3 **Foliage:** While the sky is still wet, use the round bristle brush with *light violet-gray* to add the distant trees. Add a touch of *light gray-green* to the uncleaned brush and stipple shorter foliage along the meadow line left of the gas station. Add *pastel gray-green* to the brush and paint the tall tree at the far right. Add *dark green* to the brush to make the foliage adjacent to the gas station on the left and right.

4 Switch to the fan brush and paint the meadow *pale yellow*. On both sides of the filling station just tap, tap in the color to give the illusion of grass blades. Dry.

5 Tap in a *medium green* fence row in front of the meadow on the left side of the canvas. Use the #8 round brush to add *pastel gray-green*, *dark green* and *medium green* to the foliage along the fence row.

6 **Road:** Apply *Whiteblend* to the road. While it is still wet, add horizontal streaks of *peach* and *light violet-gray;* blend. Under the shelter, use the angle brush to apply a *dark gray* shadow. Use a clean, towel-dried fan brush to soften the edge between the road and shadow. With the round brush or a corner of the fan brush, add a small *dark green* bush at the base of the shelter support. Use a clean brush to soften the lower edge of the bush into the shadow.

7 **Foreground grass:** Use the gesso brush with *dark green* to cover the foreground. Add *Green Gold* to the uncleaned brush; tap and crunch it into the wet paint to create texture. Add more *Green Gold* with a touch of *Whiteblend* and repeat, concentrating these lighter grasses in the center area and tapering them off gradually toward the sides and bottom of the canvas. Dry.

8 Load a fan brush with *Green Gold* and a touch of *Whiteblend* to crunch the final highlights in the grass; look at the finished painting for placement of the grass highlights. Do not cover all the dark green, but concentrate the brightest highlights in the center of the grass, gradually tapering them toward the sides and bottom. Add *sunny yellow* and repeat, using this color more sparingly and only in the center of the grass. Use the same colors to highlight the foliage behind the gas station.

9 **Gas station:** Remove the design protector. Add water to *dark green*, mixing to a consistency slightly thinner than *Whiteblend*. Repeat with *Burnt Sienna* and *Ultramarine Blue*. Cover the bottom section of the roof with *Clearblend*. Randomly apply the watered colors to the top of the roof and immediately add water to the bottom of the colors, letting them drip and run. Use a paper towel to keep the runs off the sky and siding. Following the angle of the roof and the pattern of missing shingles, direct the runs and pull some of the paint down, making it more transparent as it nears the bottom—let the inked lines show through. Dry. If the roof is too light, cover with *Clearblend* and touch up the color where needed.

10 Use the angle brush to paint the back of the building *off-white*. Cover the side with *Clearblend*. Brush-mix *dark gray* into *light violet-gray* to create *medium violet-gray*. Paint a brush-width horizontal shadow over the wet *Clearblend* under the side roof and a vertical shadow following the line of the corner molding at the rear of the building. Use a clean brush moistened with *Clearblend* to pull the color down and left, creating a gradual transition.

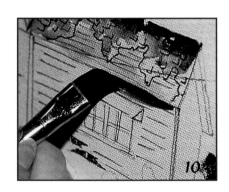

11 If the side of the building has dried, rewet it. Use the angle brush to apply translucent *light violet-gray*, allowing the inked lines to show through. Clean and dry the brush, then load one side with *Whiteblend* so that, when you hold the brush horizontally and pull toward the short side, *Whiteblend* will be on the bottom. Streak horizontally over the wet *light violet-gray*, creating clapboards. Dry. Use the liner with *dark gray* to indicate broken and missing boards. With watery *dark gray*, randomly accent some shadows under the overlaps of the boards. Dry.

12 Use the angle brush with *pale blue* to paint the windowpanes and the glass on the gas pump. Use the liner with *Whiteblend* to make the moldings on the building sides and around the windows; let dry. Use a watery *dark gray* to add shadows under the moldings. Dry. Paint the awnings with the roof colors and let dry, then add a watery, transparent shadow of *Clearblend* and a touch of *dark gray*. Soften the shadow edges.

13 Use the angle brush and *Whiteblend* to paint the wooden sign on the side of the building. Dry, then use the liner with *Monoazo Orange* to add the lettering. Use the liner brush with watery *dark gray* to make a shadow on the right side and bottom of the sign. Use differing values of *violet-gray* to paint the electric meter and *Titanium White* to paint its globe. Use the liner brush with watery *dark gray* to create a wire swooping from the meter off the right side of the canvas.

14 Brush-mix a combination of *Burnt Sienna* and *dark gray* to paint the shadows under the eaves.

15 Use the liner brush with *light violet-gray* to paint the rafters of the filling station roof. Use the angle brush with a marbleized mixture of *dark gray* and *Burnt Sienna* to paint a shadow under the roof.

16 Use a liner brush to brush-mix *dark gray* into *light violet-gray* to create *medium violet-gray*. Paint the support posts. Highlight the right sides of the posts with *Whiteblend*.

17 Paint the brick supports *Burnt Sienna* with a touch of *dark gray* on the left; highlight with *Monoazo Orange* and a touch of *Whiteblend* on the right. Create various gray values by brush-mixing *dark gray* with varying amounts of *Whiteblend*. Repeat with *Monoazo Orange*. Use these mixtures to paint the gas pump. Use a flat detail brush with light values to paint the body of the pump, placing the darkest gray on the left and the darkest orange on the right. Use the liner brush to paint the cap a brighter orange; add a medium-value gray band on top of the cap. Paint the globe *Titanium White*. Use darker and lighter gray values to paint the concrete base, the water can and the sign over the pump. Use the liner with *Mars Black* to paint the hose and nozzle.

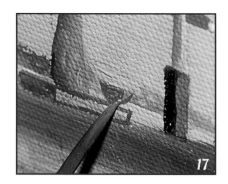

18 Use the round brush to apply *dark green* and *light gray-green* foliage along the side of the building, smudging the bottoms to "plant" them in the grass. Add *Green Gold* to the uncleaned brush and highlight the top and right side of the *dark green* foliage around the building. Protect the edge of the building with a piece of paper and highlight the dark foliage behind the building. Add *sunny yellow* to the brush to highlight only the top and right edges of the foliage. Paint the rain barrel *Burnt Sienna*, highlighting the right side with *Monoazo Orange*. Shadow the left side *dark gray*. Paint the rust lines *dark gray*.

19 Paint the "76" sign *Monoazo Orange*. While it is still wet, add a hint of *dark gray* shadow on the left and bottom areas; add a touch of *Whiteblend* to the top and right sides. Blend. Paint the numbers *Ultramarine Blue*.

20 Double load the liner brush with *medium violet-gray* and *Whiteblend* to paint the fence and signpost; dry. Highlight the right sides of the posts. Paint the wire and birds with watery *medium violet-gray*. Add flying birds to the sky.

21 Paint the "Burma Shave" sign *light violet-gray*. While it is still wet, streak with *Whiteblend* and shadow with *dark gray*. When the sign is dry, use the liner brush with *Mars Black* to add the lettering.

22 With *Whiteblend* on the liner brush, paint the bench under the filling station roof. Create the blue "road sideum" flowers by stippling *Whiteblend* and *Ultramarine Blue* with a corner of the fan brush. Use the liner brush with *dark green* and *light gray-green* to add a few grasses and twigs at the bottom of the canvas and around the base of the house.

Sign and think of the old days when gas was 27¢ a gallon. Spray your thoroughly dry canvas with Grumbacher Acrylic Painting Varnish.

Evening Chores

Grumbacher Artists' Acrylic Colors
Burnt Sienna
Burnt Umber
Grumbacher Gray
Monoazo Orange
Monoazo Orange (Soft
  Formula jar color)
Thalo® Crimson
Titanium White
Ultramarine Blue

Brushes
Sable Essence™ ½" angle brush
Golden Edge™ #2 liner brush
Golden Edge™ #6 round brush
Golden Edge™ #8 filbert brush
#1 Bristle Fan brush
two 2" gesso brushes
2" hake brush

Other Supplies
16"x20" stretched canvas
Grumbacher Acrylic Painting Varnish
Clearblend
Whiteblend
Slowblend
tapered painting knife
natural sponge
adhesive design protector
masking tape
graphite paper, stylus

Palette
Before you begin, prepare these color mixtures.
pale peach—Whiteblend, Monoazo Orange
pale gray—Whiteblend, Ultramarine Blue, Burnt Umber, Soft Monoazo Orange

Prepare these color mixtures as you need them.
brick—Burnt Sienna, Thalo® Crimson
maroon—Burnt Umber, Thalo® Crimson
violet-gray—pale gray, Ultramarine Blue, Burnt Umber, Thalo® Crimson
light blue—Whiteblend, Ultramarine Blue
brilliant orange—Monoazo Orange, touch of Whiteblend
navy—Ultramarine Blue, Grumbacher Gray
dusty brown—Burnt Umber, pale gray

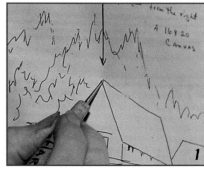

1 Background: Transfer only the tree line, barn and hillside to your canvas. Place an adhesive design protector over the barn. While painting, make sure to brush away from the adhesive.

2 Using a gesso brush loaded with *pale peach*, cover the sky and tree area. While this area is still wet, use the uncleaned brush to apply *pale gray* horizontally across the top of the sky. Blend thoroughly; don't clean the brush yet. Do the final blending with a light dusting stroke of the hake brush.

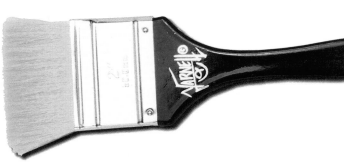

3 **Foliage:** For the most distant row of trees, use a combination of *pale peach* and *pale gray*. Apply this mixture with the fan brush turned vertically, tapping the brush and pulling it downward so it touches the top of the meadow. While this is still wet, use the uncleaned gesso brush to blend the bottom edges, creating a foggy mist between the meadow line and distant trees.

4 Use the fan brush with *pale gray* to make a second, shorter row of trees in front of the distant tree line. For trees shorter than the width of the fan brush, hold the brush horizontally. Add a touch of *Grumbacher Gray* to your uncleaned brush and use the same technique to paint a third, darker row in front of the second row, taking care that it joins the top of the meadow. Do not mist the bottoms of these trees.

5 To make the trees behind the barn, add *Burnt Umber, maroon* and *brick*, alternately, to the uncleaned fan brush. Hold the brush vertically to gently tap in the tall trees. Use the corner of the brush to make the short foliage.

6 Use the corner of a clean fan brush to apply *Whiteblend* highlights on the tops and left sides of some trees and some in the foliage to separate the trees. Use a clean moist sponge to remove excess paint from the meadow at the base of the trees. Dry.

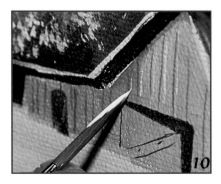

7   **Barns:** Remove the adhesive protector. Alternating between the large and small barns, follow steps 7–10 to paint a section of the large barn, then add pale gray to each color and use the lightened color to paint the corresponding part of the distant barn. Cover the bottom half of the roof with *Clearblend*. Use an angle brush to apply *Burnt Sienna* to the top half of the roof. Accent the wet *Burnt Sienna* with dabs of *brick, maroon* and *Grumbacher Gray*. Use a clean brush moistened with *Clearblend* to blend the bottom of this area into the wet *Clearblend* on the lower half of the roof. Paint the side of the barn maroon.

8   Use a liner brush loaded with *maroon* and a touch of *Grumbacher Gray* to create eaves on the large barn. Load a combination of *violet-gray* and *peach* with a touch of *brick* onto the angle brush and paint the entire barn front. Highlight the right side of the front by blending more *Whiteblend* into the wet paint in that area. Leave the left side of the barn front darker. Dry.

9   Use a liner brush to add *Whiteblend* snow on both roofs; gently pull down with the liner to make icicles.

10   Use the liner with watery *violet-gray* to paint the details on the barn front. Use a mixture of *maroon* and *Grumbacher Gray* to paint the shadow inside the door opening. Use a watery mixture of the same colors for the details.

11   Use the gesso brush with *Whiteblend* to apply the snow base to the distant meadow. Use the fan brush to alternately streak *pale gray* and *violet-gray* across the wet canvas. Use *violet-gray* on the flat bristle brush to establish the top of the foreground meadow. Use a gesso brush to cover the remaining foreground with *Whiteblend*. Blend the *Whiteblend* into the *violet-gray*. Darken the bottom of the foreground with *Grumbacher Gray*, *Ultramarine Blue* and *brick*. To indicate shadows in the drifting snow, use the fan brush to add streaks of *violet-gray* in the remaining wet *Whiteblend*. Blend with a clean gesso brush. Dry thoroughly.

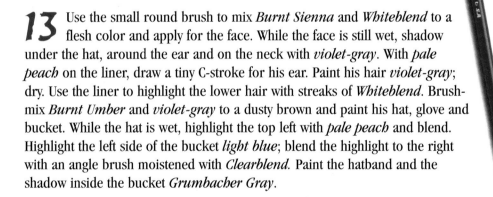

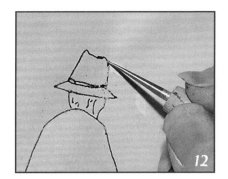

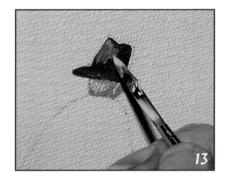

12 **Grandpa:** Transfer Grandpa so the bottoms of his feet rest on the crest of the hill.

13 Use the small round brush to mix *Burnt Sienna* and *Whiteblend* to a flesh color and apply for the face. While the face is still wet, shadow under the hat, around the ear and on the neck with *violet-gray*. With *pale peach* on the liner, draw a tiny C-stroke for his ear. Paint his hair *violet-gray*; dry. Use the liner to highlight the lower hair with streaks of *Whiteblend*. Brush-mix *Burnt Umber* and *violet-gray* to a dusty brown and paint his hat, glove and bucket. While the hat is wet, highlight the top left with *pale peach* and blend. Highlight the left side of the bucket *light blue*; blend the highlight to the right with an angle brush moistened with *Clearblend.* Paint the hatband and the shadow inside the bucket *Grumbacher Gray.*

14 Add a few drops of *Slowblend* to *Monoazo Orange, maroon* and *brick.* Paint and blend one section of the jacket at a time, using *Monoazo Orange* in the lightest areas, *brick* in the middle of each section and *maroon* in the shaded areas. Work quickly to prevent the paint from lifting in spots. Dry. Cover a section with *Clearblend;* while it is still wet, highlight the left side with *brilliant orange.* Touch up imperfections in the first coat and deepen the shadows with more *maroon.* Blend the additions with a brush moistened with *Clearblend.* Repeat for each section.

15 Use the angle brush to paint his overalls one section at a time with *navy.* While the base coat is still wet, highlight the left side and fabric folds with *light blue* on the liner brush. Blend with a clean, towel-dried filbert brush.

16 Cover a section of the overalls with *Clearblend.* Go over the pants colors again, redefining highlights, shadows and folds as you did for the coat.

17 Use the angle and filbert brushes with *Grumbacher Gray* to paint Grandpa's boots. Highlight the left back of each boot with *pale gray*; blend. While his boots are still wet, apply a touch of *Whiteblend* to the bottom of the right sole. Paint the cane with the liner brush and watery *Grumbacher Gray*.

18 **Snow details:** Add details to one section at a time, allowing for changes and wiping away any mistakes. Apply *Clearblend* over the area of the snow where Grandpa's tracks will be. With your fan brush, place irregular tracks of *violet-gray* at the crest of the hill behind his boots, keeping them close together near the boots and spacing them farther apart as they move toward the edge of the canvas.

19 Using a clean fan brush moistened with *Clearblend*, soften the edges and fade out the tracks. Add clumps of snow with *Titanium White* and *Whiteblend*. Smooth away any unwanted hard edges with a clean brush moistened with *Clearblend*.

20 Apply the distant grasses with a fan brush and watery *dusty brown*. Create shadows by stroking the bottom of the wet grass to the right and along the angle of the hill. Tuck the grass into the snow by adding a clump of snow to the left of the grass. Blot the bottom of the snow to "plant" the grass.

21 Continue adding patches of grass throughout. Darken them as you move closer to the bottom by adding *Burnt Umber* to the uncleaned fan brush. In the foreground, turn the brush vertically and tap the corner gently against the canvas to create foliage in some grass clusters. As before, smudge the bottoms and add snow clumps to plant the grasses. With the liner brush and *Burnt Umber*, lift up a few tall blades. Dry.

22 Use a fan brush to spatter watery *Whiteblend* over the canvas. Pat with a clean moist sponge. Dry the canvas and spatter again, but this time don't pat with the sponge. Dry again and repeat as often as you like.

Sign and reminisce! When the painting is completely dry, spray with Grumbacher Acrylic Painting Varnish.

Heritage

Grumbacher Artists' Acrylic Colors
Burnt Sienna
Burnt Umber
Cadmium Yellow Medium
Mars Black
Monoazo Orange
Thio™ Violet
  (Quinacridone Magenta)
Titanium White
Ultramarine Blue
Yellow Ochre Light

Brushes
Golden Edge™ #8 filbert brush
Sable Essence™ ½" angle brush
Golden Edge™ #2 liner brush
Multi-Texture brush
2" gesso brush

Other Supplies
16"x20" stretched canvas
Grumbacher Acrylic Painting Varnish
Whiteblend
Slowblend
tapered painting knife
natural sponge
Rapidograph technical pen #2.00
Rotring Artist Ink: transparent brown
16"x20" mat template (11½"x15½"
  opening)
masking tape
graphite paper, stylus

Palette
Before you begin, prepare these color mixtures.
pale yellow—Yellow Ochre Light, Whiteblend
pale peach—Whiteblend, Monoazo Orange
light blue—Whiteblend, Ultramarine Blue
grape—Burnt Umber, Thio™ Violet, Ultramarine Blue,
  Whiteblend

Prepare these color mixtures as you need them.
bright yellow—Whiteblend, Cadmium Yellow Medium
maroon—6 parts Burnt Sienna, 2 parts Burnt Umber,
  1 part Thio™ Violet
warm brown—3 parts Burnt Umber, 1 part Burnt
  Sienna, 1 part Slowblend
light gray—Whiteblend, Burnt Sienna, Ultramarine
  Blue, Burnt Umber

1 **Background:** With a gesso brush, base coat the canvas *light gray* and dry. Line up the mat template with the edges of the canvas and hold it firmly in place. Use the pen with brown ink to draw a border around the inside of the mat opening.

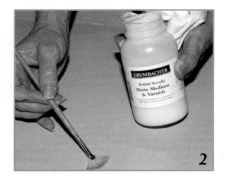

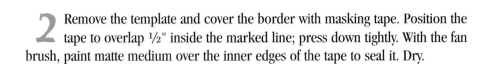

2 Remove the template and cover the border with masking tape. Position the tape to overlap ½" inside the marked line; press down tightly. With the fan brush, paint matte medium over the inner edges of the tape to seal it. Dry.

3 Using the gesso brush, cover the area inside the tape with *Clearblend*. Starting at the top while the canvas is still wet and using the same uncleaned brush, apply successive bands first of *pale yellow*, then *pale peach*, *light blue* and *grape* over the wet *Clearblend*. Use a clean, dry fan brush to blend the edges slightly where they join. Pat to blend with a clean, moist sponge, creating texture and a gradual transition between colors.

4 Use the sponge to apply more of the same colors, if needed in any area. Keep the dark colors along the bottom of the masked-off area and filling the lower left corner. Pat to blend one color into the next, creating a gradual transition. If the paint begins to lift, stop and dry the canvas. Rewet with *Clearblend* and repeat. Dry thoroughly.

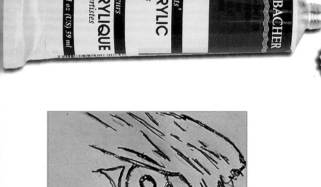

5 Transfer the eagle pattern, placing the center of the eye 5¼" from the top of the canvas and 8" from the right edge.

Remember When, page 36

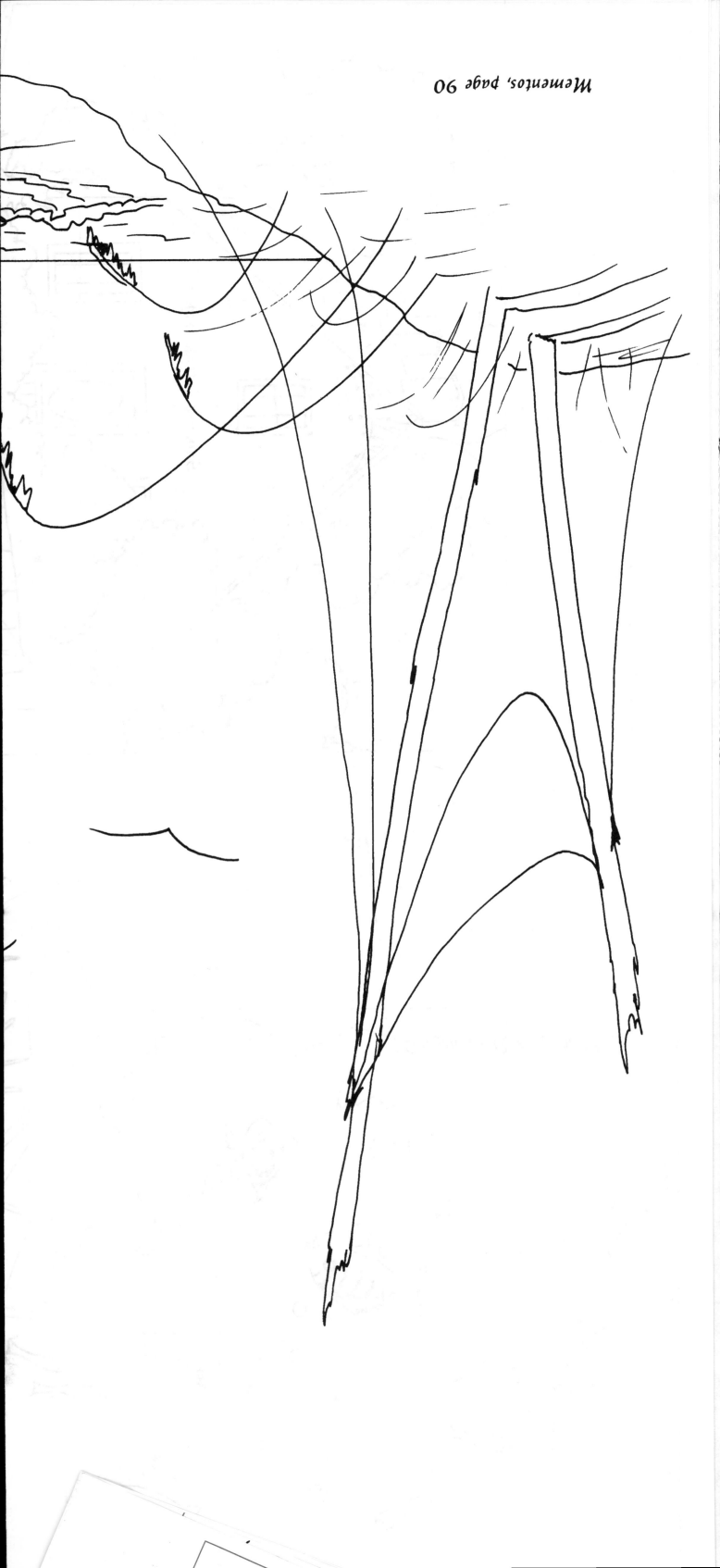

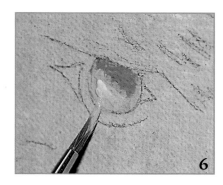

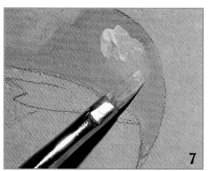

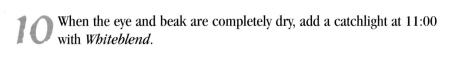

6 **Eye and beak:** Use a liner brush with *Yellow Ochre Light* to paint the iris of the eye, eyelids and eye socket. While it's still wet, add a touch of *Whiteblend* to the bottom rim of the iris and blend slightly. Dry thoroughly and highlight with *bright yellow*.

7 The beak consists of three parts: the upper and lower mandibles and the cere, the fleshy band which connects the back of the upper mandible with the head. With the angle brush, paint the upper mandible and cere *Yellow Ochre Light*, connecting the cere to the eye socket. Highlight, shadow and blend wet-on-wet. Place a *pale yellow* highlight in the center of the upper beak, then use the liner to draw a thin *pale yellow* line along the side. Add a *bright yellow* highlight near the top of the cere and blend it in. Place a *maroon* shadow where the cere connects to the upper beak and on the sharp point. Pat to blend—do not overblend; the beak has many imperfections.

8 Cover the eye and socket with *Clearblend.* While this is wet, use the liner brush with a mixture of *maroon* and *Clearblend* to outline and shadow the eye. Create a V-shaped corner between the eye and cere. Darken the eye socket with a watery mixture of *maroon* and a touch of *Mars Black.* Use this darkened maroon on the liner brush for the wrinkles around the eye. Use the liner to paint the pupil *Mars Black.*

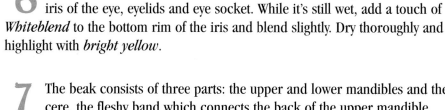

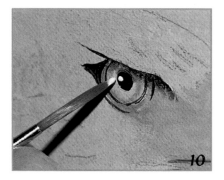

9 With the Multi-Texture brush, paint the underside of the beak *Yellow Ochre Light.* While the beak is still wet add a *maroon* shadow and a *pale yellow* highlight line along the side, creating a ridge near the edge. Blend. Cover both mandibles with *Clearblend.* Touch up the shadows if needed; add a *bright yellow* highlight in the center of the upper mandible. Pat to blend while it is still wet.

10 When the eye and beak are completely dry, add a catchlight at 11:00 with *Whiteblend*.

11 Using the Multi-Texture brush lightly loaded with *maroon,* lightly tap the area under the eye and corner of the cere to create "hair" growing from the fleshy area in front of the eye.

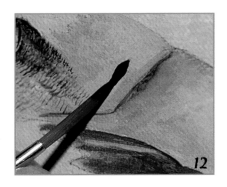

12 Load the liner brush with a watery mixture of *maroon* and *Mars Black* to add an oval nostril to the beak.

13 **Body:** Use the picture of the finished body as a guide for dark color placement. Do not allow the body paint to extend to the tape, but blend gradually so it disappears before reaching the tape. Cover the bottom and left side of the canvas with a mixture of *Clearblend* and *Slowblend*. Apply this mixture in the light areas on each section of the body to assist you in graduating the color. Apply and work the body paint while the *Clearblend/Slowblend* is wet—if it dries, add more in the area that you are working. Use the angle brush to apply *warm brown* in the dark area of the most distant wing. Immediately brush over the *warm brown* with a Multi-Texture brush moistened with *Clearblend,* making C-strokes to create feather markings and a gradual transition of color value. Next paint the neck section, then the chest.

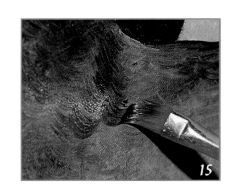

14 Check to see if the bottom and left corner of the canvas are still wet; if they are beginning to dry, reapply *Clearblend/Slowblend.* Wet the light areas of the foreground wing with the mixture also. Apply *warm brown* into the dark areas of the wing.

15 Using the *Clearblend*-moistened Multi-Texture brush, create feather texture in the light, medium and dark areas of the foreground wing. Add more *Clearblend/Slowblend* to fade any hard edges; do not overblend. The color will begin to lift in spots as it gets tacky. Dry. Touch-ups are much easier wet-on-dry. Wet-on-sticky is tricky!

16 **Head and feathers:** Using the angle brush with *grape,* follow the pattern lines to base coat general shape of the darkest, shadowed or recessed areas of the eagle's head and neck. Add a touch of *Whiteblend* to the uncleaned brush and fill in the rest of the head and neck with choppy feather strokes, leaving the *grape* dark in the darkest shadow areas.

17 Look at the finished painting for the placement of feather highlights. Notice the direction of growth and the length of the feathers and adjust your feather strokes accordingly. For the small, short feathers around the eye, beak and forehead, use a filbert brush. Use the angle brush for the longer feathers. Add a touch more *Whiteblend* to your uncleaned brush and randomly apply choppy feather strokes throughout the wet base coat. Add more *Whiteblend* and continue, this time concentrating in the areas that will be lightest when finished: the top of the head, the center of the cheek, and the center neck area.

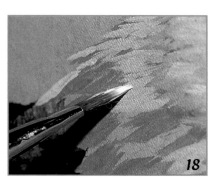

18 Highlight the feathers with a clean brush and *Whiteblend,* still using choppy feather strokes. Do not cover all the *grape;* allow it to show among the white feathers throughout the head and neck. Be careful to keep the contours of the bird, retaining the deep shadow under the head and the recessed areas around the face. Occasionally blot the feathers to remove paint from the shadows cast by the feathers above—leave the tips white. With a clean brush and *Titanium White,* add the brightest highlights to the center of the cheek, the center of the neck and the top of the head. Dry.

19 For the distinct feathers overlapping the body, use the Multi-Texture brush and thinned *Whiteblend* to add the detailed edges. Don't paint the details perfectly; paint only half of some feathers and make some scruffy ones. Randomly add a few in the neck area. Continue with the same brush to add hair-like feather marks on the head. Begin at the cere and lightly tap back across the face. To correct an area or add shadow, cover with *Clearblend,* then add the needed touch-up. Soften the edges with the Multi-Texture brush moistened with *Clearblend.*

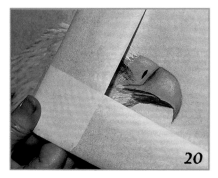

20 After your painting is thoroughly dry, remove the masking tape by gently pulling in the direction of the canvas.

Sign and soar with the eagles! When the painting is thoroughly dry, spray with Grumbacher Acrylic Painting Varnish.

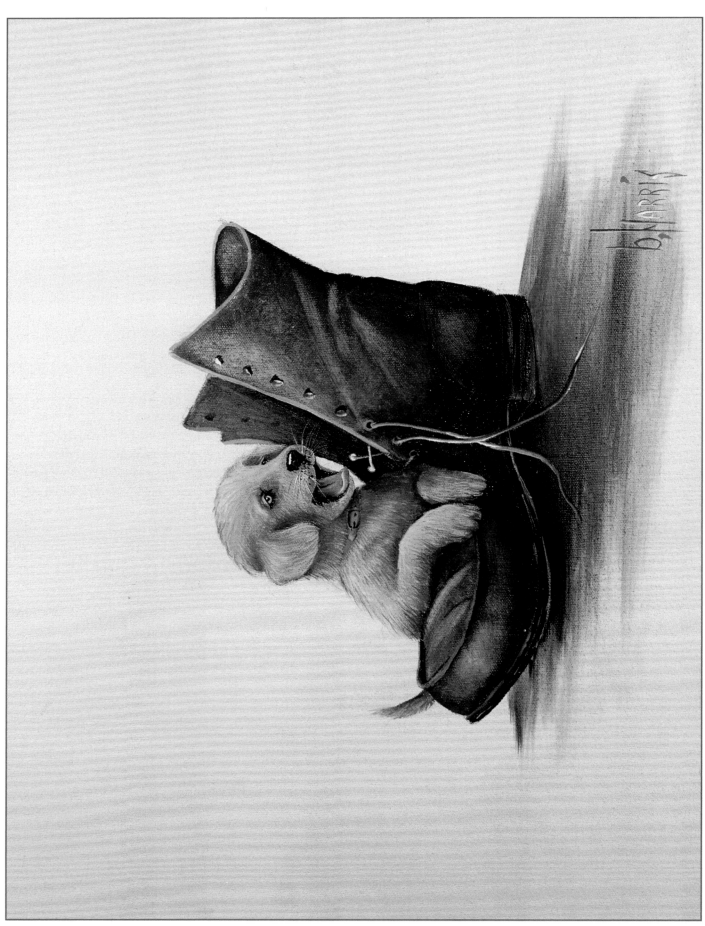

7 Use the liner brush and alternate *watery tan* and *medium brown* to add the detail lines lines on the heel and sole. Create the raised seam around the toe with the liner and *dark brown*. Use the liner with *tan* to highlight the seam.

8 **Puppy:** Apply a thin wash of *Raw Sienna* over the iris in each eye. Dry. Highlight the bottom of the iris with *Cadmium Yellow Medium* and *Whiteblend*. Blend.

9 Observe the finished painting for the placement of dark and light areas. Notice the darkest shadows are around the eyes, ears, chin and chest. Cover one section at a time with *Clearblend* and, while it is wet, apply a scruffy base coat of *light brown, medium brown* and *dark brown,* blending where the colors overlap. Also blend between adjacent sections. Apply translucent *light brown* to the lightest area, *dark brown* to the darkest area, and *medium brown* in between, blending where they overlap. Keep the colors translucent, not opaque as for the boot—rather, leave a glow from the canvas and the shadow markings showing through. Dry.

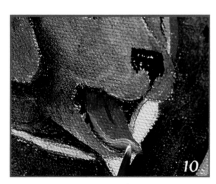

10 Paint the puppy's tongue *medium pink* and shadow with *dark brown*. Highlight the side and tip with *light yellow*. Blend the colors slightly with the liner brush. Dry. With the liner brush and watery *dark brown,* add a thin line down the center of his tongue.

11 Moisten the area around the eyes with *Clearblend*. While the area is wet, use the liner brush to add more *dark brown* shadow to accent the eyes. Use the Multi-Texture brush moistened with *Clearblend* to gradually fade the color. Fill in the collar with *Cadmium Red Light*. (The collar details will be added when the puppy is completely dry.)

12 As you paint the fur, keep in mind the fur length and direction of growth in each area. For example, the muzzle fur is extremely short; indicate this by tapping those areas with the Multi-Texture brush and the highlight color. Make longer strokes as you move away from the face.

13 The fur highlight colors are *medium rust, medium yellow, bright yellow* and *light yellow*. Thin them to a thinner consistency than *Whiteblend*. The fur highlights should always be a value lighter than the base coat; if they do not show, lighten the color. Apply the first three highlight colors with the Multi-Texture brush, placing *medium rust* primarily in the shadowed areas, *bright yellow* in the lightest areas and *medium yellow* in between. Use very light pressure on the brush, allowing the base color to show through the fur.

14 Use the liner with all four highlight colors to add "scruffy" fur strokes. Apply a final *light yellow* highlight to the head, ear, shoulder, feet and legs. Touch up as needed by alternating the highlight colors. Use the liner with *light yellow* to add a brow over each eye, fading each end with a brush moistened with *Clearblend*. When the puppy is completely dry, if it needs more shadow, mix a watery, transparent wash of *dark brown*, *Clearblend* and water. Use this mix as needed to strengthen the shadows and add a shadow on the boot under the puppy. If the puppy is too "chalky," lightly brush a watery wash of *Clearblend*, *Yellow Ochre Light* and water over the puppy with the Multi-Texture brush. Dry.

15 Use the liner brush with *Mars Black* to stipple the whisker dots on the muzzle. Add the whiskers with the pen or with the liner and watery *Mars Black*. Highlight a few spots on some whiskers.

16 With the liner brush loaded with *Titanium White*, paint a catchlight across the top of his nose and one in each eye.

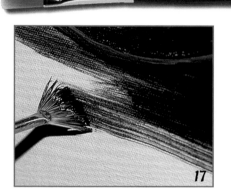

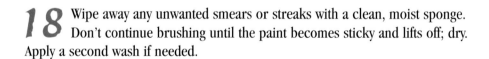

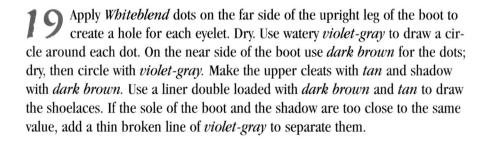

17 **Boot shadow:** With a very moist gesso brush, apply a mixture of *Slowblend* and *Clearblend* around the bottom and sides of the canvas, overlapping into where the shadows are to be painted. Use a fan brush to apply a *dark brown* shadow close to, but smaller than, the boot. Brush the edges horizontally out into the wet *Slowblend/Clearblend,* gradually fading them into the clear.

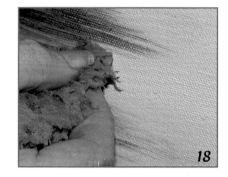

18 Wipe away any unwanted smears or streaks with a clean, moist sponge. Don't continue brushing until the paint becomes sticky and lifts off; dry. Apply a second wash if needed.

19 Apply *Whiteblend* dots on the far side of the upright leg of the boot to create a hole for each eyelet. Dry. Use watery *violet-gray* to draw a circle around each dot. On the near side of the boot use *dark brown* for the dots; dry, then circle with *violet-gray.* Make the upper cleats with *tan* and shadow with *dark brown.* Use a liner double loaded with *dark brown* and *tan* to draw the shoelaces. If the sole of the boot and the shadow are too close to the same value, add a thin broken line of *violet-gray* to separate them.

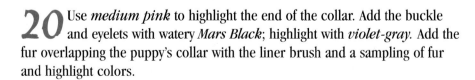

20 Use *medium pink* to highlight the end of the collar. Add the buckle and eyelets with watery *Mars Black*; highlight with *violet-gray.* Add the fur overlapping the puppy's collar with the liner brush and a sampling of fur and highlight colors.

Sign and dry thoroughly. Spray the finished painting with Grumbacher Acrylic Painting Varnish, put on your old boots and go for a walk with your new friend!

Summer Cottage

Grumbacher Artists' Acrylic Colors
Cadmium Yellow Medium
Cerulean Blue
Chromium Oxide Green
Cobalt Titanate Green
Grumbacher Gray
Grumbacher Red (Naphthol Red)
Mars Black
Monoazo Orange
Thalo® Green
Thio™ Violet (Quinacridone Magenta)
Titanium White
Ultramarine Blue

Brushes
Eterna #8 & #12 round bristle brushes
Gainsborough® #6 flat bristle brush
Professional™ #6 bristle filbert brush
Sable Essence™ ½" angle brush
Golden Edge™ #2 liner brush
#1 Bristle Fan brush
2" hake brush
2" gesso brush

other supplies
16"x20" stretched canvas
Grumbacher Acrylic Painting Varnish
Clearblend
Whiteblend
tapered painting knife
natural sponge
masking tape
graphite paper, stylus

Palette

Before you begin, prepare these color mixtures.
sky blue—Cerulean Blue, Whiteblend
sky gray—Whiteblend, Cerulean Blue, Monoazo Orange
peach—Whiteblend, Monoazo Orange
off-white—Titanium White, Monoazo Orange, Cadmium Yellow Medium
dark green—4 parts Grumbacher Gray, 1 part Thalo® Green
light gray-green—sky gray, touch of dark green
black-green—Thalo® Green, Mars Black

Prepare these color mixtures as you need them.
violet-gray—Ultramarine Blue, Grumbacher Gray, Thio™ Violet, Whiteblend
dark brown—Mars Black, Monoazo Orange marbleized
terra cotta—Whiteblend, Monoazo Orange, Grumbacher Gray
bright peach—peach, Monoazo Orange
pale violet—Thio™ Violet, Titanium White
pale pink—Titanium White, Grumbacher Red
dark gray—Grumbacher Gray, Whiteblend

These colors are to be brush-mixed as needed.
pastel green—Cobalt Titanate Green, touch of sky gray
yellow-green—Cobalt Titanate Green, Whiteblend, touch of Cadmium Yellow Medium

1 **Sky:** Use a gesso brush to paint the top ⅓ of your canvas *sky blue*. While it's wet, add *sky gray* to the brush and place irregular cloud shapes in the center of the canvas. Blend the edges with the dry hake brush. Dry. Highlight and blend one cloud puff at a time. Generously load the bristle filbert brush with *Clearblend* and dab excess on a paper towel. Load a corner of the fan brush with *peach* and *off-white* for highlights. Dab on the top edge of a cloud, then immediately pat, pat with the filbert, redistributing highlights into the cloud. Move gradually inward with each pat to create a transition. Dab a highlight in each cloud center and pat around the edges. Clean and reload the filbert brush often. Repeat highlighting and blending until you have the degree of cloudiness you want.

2 Foliage: Load the #12 round brush with *light gray-green* and tap in the distant trees on the right side of the canvas. Add a touch of *black-green* to the uncleaned brush and stipple in the middle trees.

3 The group of trees in the canvas center is 4½" from the top and 5½" from each side. With *black-green* on the #12 round brush, apply the irregularly shaped top of these trees. Load the gesso brush with *black-green* and solidly fill the bottom of the canvas, connecting the color to the trees. Dry thoroughly.

4 Transfer the house and fence, placing the fence top 8" above the canvas bottom. Sketch the path starting 4" above the bottom. With the sponge, mix *Chromium Oxide Green* and *Ultramarine Blue*; lightly tap the canvas to paint tiny speckles of reflected light throughout the foliage. Add *light gray-green* to the uncleaned sponge and tap around in an irregular pattern, defining the top and outer edges of the foliage in front of the fence and around the path.

5 Path: Load the flat bristle brush with *dark brown* and apply horizontal strokes, leaving the edges ragged. Make the strokes wider as you move toward the bottom of the canvas. Add *Monoazo Orange* to your brush and blend over the *dark brown*.

6 While the canvas is still wet, streak *peach* and *off-white* onto the path with the fan brush. Make the strokes wider as you move toward the bottom of the canvas. Leave the left side of the path darker than the right. Blend the edges; do not overblend.

7 To create rounded highlights on the *black-green* foliage on the trees and the bushes in front of the fence, brush mix the highlight colors at the same time as you load the #8 round brush by tapping up and down straight into the colors on the palette, slightly flaring the bristles.

Lightly stipple the highlights onto the foliage, beginning with the dullest highlights of *pastel green*; apply this about ¾ of the way around each foliage cluster. Should you apply a blob, blot the bottom to subdue and "plant" it. Leave lots of *black-green* unpainted. Save space for the flowers below the fence. Use *yellow-green* for the middle value highlights. For the final highlights, add *peach* to the uncleaned brush. Apply sparingly and only on the top left edges. Dry.

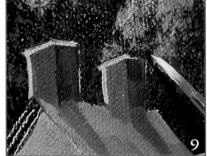

8 **Cottage:** Base coat the front (sunny) side of the cottage using *sky blue* along the right corner and *sky gray* over the remainder. On the right (shadow) side, apply *sky blue* on the right and *violet-gray* on the left. Blend and dry. With a clean angle brush, paint the roof *terra cotta*. While the roof is still wet, apply a *bright peach* highlight at the top, fading the color to the bottom. With the liner brush and a mixture of *peach* and *terra cotta*, apply the left edge of the roof. Dry.

9 Use the angle brush with *Monoazo Orange* to paint the chimneys. Add a touch of *Mars Black* to your brush to shadow the right sides. Add *Clearblend* to the uncleaned brush and add a transparent shadow on the roof behind each chimney. Load the liner brush with *bright peach* to highlight the top and left side of each chimney. Dry thoroughly.

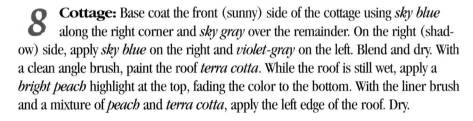

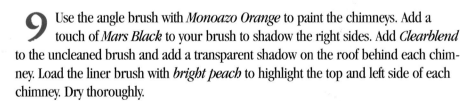

10 Cover the front of the house with *Clearblend*. While this is wet, use the angle brush to apply a diagonal patch of *off-white* to highlight along the eave on the left side. With a clean towel-dried angle brush, blend and fade the colors diagonally to the right. Using a mixture of *Clearblend* and *violet-gray* on the corner of the fan brush, dabble an irregularly shaped shadow from the foliage on the left corner of the house. Use the angle brush with the same mixture to add a shadow at the peak of the roof. Use *violet-gray* on the angle brush to paint the windows and doors. Dry.

11 Use the liner brush and *Whiteblend* to apply the window, door and gingerbread moldings; dry. Add *violet-gray* shadows along the bottoms and right sides of the moldings and above and to the right of the shrubbery.

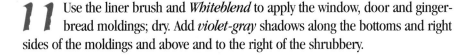

12 Use the fan brush with *Clearblend* to cover the bottom of the fence where it disappears behind the foliage. Base coat the fence using vertical strokes of the flat brush—alternate between *sky blue* and *sky gray* on the front, and use *violet-gray* on the side fence. Use less pressure on the brush as you paint downward so the fence becomes translucent and gradually disappears into shadow behind the foliage. While it is still wet, blot to remove all sharp edges. Dry.

13 Cover the fence with *Clearblend.* While it is wet, randomly add vertical accent dashes of *pale pink* and *pale violet.* With the flat brush and *off-white,* add highlights along the top center of the fence, using longer strokes in the gate area ending at the corner. Slightly moisten a clean angle brush with *Clearblend* and create a gradual transition at the bottom of the highlight. Dry. Use the liner with watery *dark gray* to divide the planks.

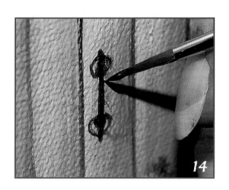

14 Load the liner brush with *Grumbacher Gray* to paint the handle and hinge on the gate.

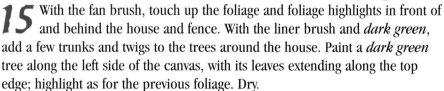

15 With the fan brush, touch up the foliage and foliage highlights in front of and behind the house and fence. With the liner brush and *dark green*, add a few trunks and twigs to the trees around the house. Paint a *dark green* tree along the left side of the canvas, with its leaves extending along the top edge; highlight as for the previous foliage. Dry.

16 Use the #8 round brush to stipple in a *dark green* branch extending from the tree in front of the fence. Use the liner brush to add a few *black-green* leaves and to highlight some leaves with *yellow-green.*

17 Clean the liner brush. Double load it with *dark gray* and *off-white* to paint the distant birds.

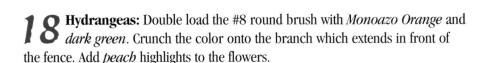

18 **Hydrangeas:** Double load the #8 round brush with *Monoazo Orange* and *dark green*. Crunch the color onto the branch which extends in front of the fence. Add *peach* highlights to the flowers.

19 To make the hydrangeas in shadow by the fence and in the bottom corners, brush mix *Ultramarine Blue* and *Cerulean Blue* with a touch of *Grumbacher Red*. Add a touch of *Whiteblend* and apply highlights on the top left. Use *Ultramarine Blue* and *Titanium White* for the hydrangeas along the path, highlighting them with a mix of *Cerulean Blue* and *Titanium White*. Paint a few small brush-mixed *yellow-green* and *pastel green* leaves among the flowers.

20 **Grass and flowers:** Place a few clusters of *yellow-green* grass and leaves throughout the foreground foliage. Add *pastel green* to the brush and paint the flower stems. Double load the liner brush with *peach* and *Monoazo Orange* to add small circular flowers on top of the stems. When the flowers are dry, add *dark brown* centers.

21 Use the bristle filbert brush to tap in a *black-green* base for the hollyhock leaves. Dry and load the liner brush with *Grumbacher Red* to do the blossoms. First add *Whiteblend* to the uncleaned brush for more round flowers, then add *Monoazo Orange* and repeat. Tap in a few small *yellow-green* and *pastel green* leaves. Add more leaves throughout the garden foliage with a variety of green shades, brush-mixing as you go.

22 Use the corner of the fan brush to paint the *Thio*™ *Violet* flowers along the path. Add *Titanium White* to your brush to highlight.

Sign and stroll through the garden to the cottage next door! When your painting is thoroughly dry, spray with Grumbacher Acrylic Painting Varnish.

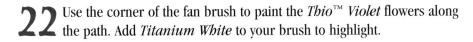

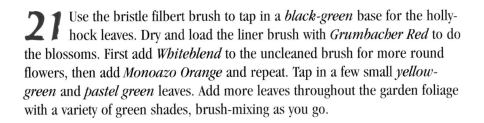

Off the Beaten Path

Grumbacher Artists' Acrylic Colors
Burnt Sienna
Burnt Umber
Hooker's Green
Monoazo Orange
Ultramarine Blue
Yellow Ochre Light

Brushes
Eterna #8 & #12 round bristle brushes
Golden Edge™ #6 flat detail brush
Golden Edge™ #1 liner brush
two 2" gesso brushes
#1 Bristle Fan brush

Other Supplies
16"x20" stretched canvas
Grumbacher Acrylic Painting Varnish
Clearblend
Whiteblend
tapered painting knife
natural sponge
masking tape
graphite paper, stylus

Palette
Before you begin, prepare these color mixtures.
pink—Whiteblend, Monoazo Orange
sky blue—Whiteblend, Ultramarine Blue
blue-gray—4 parts Ultramarine Blue, 1 part Monoazo
  Orange, 1 part Whiteblend
light blue-gray—blue-gray, Whiteblend
dark gray—5 parts Ultramarine Blue, 1 part Monoazo
  Orange, 1 part blue-gray
light green—light blue-gray, touch of Yellow Ochre
  Light

Prepare these color mixtures as you need them.
dark tree green—3 parts Ultramarine Blue, 1 part
  Burnt Umber, 1 part Hooker's Green
peach—Whiteblend, Monoazo Orange
light yellow—Whiteblend, Yellow Ochre Light
medium green—dark tree green, Whiteblend; touch
  of Yellow Ochre
yellow-green—medium green, Yellow Ochre Light,
  Whiteblend
terra cotta—yellow-green, Yellow Ochre Light,
  Monoazo Orange, Whiteblend

1 **Background:** Transfer the design to the canvas, off-centered to the right, placing the barn bottom 4" from the bottom of the canvas and the distant meadow line ¾" higher. Before you begin painting, cover the barn with an adhesive protector. Load the gesso brush with *pink* and generously cover the top ⅔ of the canvas. While this is still wet, add streaks of *sky blue* across the top and blend with a dry gesso brush. Using the #8 round brush, tap in a distant tree line with *light blue-gray*. While the trees are still wet, use a fan brush to mist the bottoms with *peach*.

1

2 Add *light green* to the uncleaned #8 round brush and, following the pattern lines, tap in the middle tree line so it sits on the distant meadow.

3 Use the fan brush with *light yellow* to paint the meadow, overlapping the bottom of the tree line.

4 **Foliage:** Create the large cluster of trees by tapping in *blue-gray* with the #12 round brush, giving them an irregular, lacy edge. Add more *dark gray* to the uncleaned brush as you move down toward the barn. Do not go all the way to the barn with *blue-gray*.

5 Load the painting knife with *dark tree green* and spread onto the canvas to form the center of the foliage.

6 With the #12 round brush, stipple the wet *dark tree green* over the inside edges of the *blue-gray*, creating a gradual transition between the two colors and foliage texture in the *dark tree green*. With the same brush, add a few low bushes on each side of the trees. Dry.

7 Randomly tap *medium green* highlights throughout the tree area with the #8 round bristle brush. Apply the highlights with a gentle touch, creating leafy areas but always leaving some dark base showing. The *yellow-green* highlights should be more precisely placed to create clusters of foliage. The brightest areas will be the top and left sides of each cluster. This color continues about two-thirds of the way around each cluster and become less dense as you move toward the right side of each.

8 Add *terra cotta* to the dirty brush and highlight the top and left edges of a few clusters on the left side. The right side should remain dull. Add a touch more Yellow Ochre Light to your uncleaned brush and highlight the very tops and edges of the foliage.

9 **Meadow:** To create depth in the foreground, alternate between light and dark colors, connecting them. Begin at the top of the meadow with a fan brush loaded with *light yellow*. Tap the color over the bottom of the dark foreground foliage. Add *dark tree green* to your uncleaned brush and overlap only the bottom of the *light yellow* grass on the left of the barn, creating a shadow. With a medium-value mix of *dark tree green* and *light yellow*, establish the top of the foreground meadow on the left of the canvas, connecting it to the foliage base. Use two gesso brushes to paint the foreground grass. Load one with *light yellow*; apply horizontally through the meadow center. With the other, paint the meadow bottom *dark tree green*. Create texture and a gradual transition by crunching the uncleaned brushes into the wet areas. Crunch *peach* texture and accents into the *light yellow* areas. Where dark and light connect, crunch light in the dark and dark in the light, creating a middle value. Crunch the middle value on each side of the meadow to frame the light center. Crunch with a clean fan brush to soften unwanted sharp color transitions.

10 Load the fan brush with *dark tree green*. Following the lines traced onto your canvas, push the color along each side of the canvas and along the right side of the barn.

11 **Barn:** Remove the adhesive protector. Apply *Clearblend* across the bottom half of the roof. Apply a mixture of *Burnt Sienna* with a touch of *Monoazo Orange* to the top third of the roof.

12 To create a gradual transition from dark to light, use the fan brush moistened with *Clearblend* to pull the color from the top of the roof into the *Clearblend*. Blend.

13 Use the same technique for the sides of the barn, but with *Burnt Umber* and a touch of *dark tree green*. Load the detail brush with the combination and start at the corner of the front side of the barn. Add *Clearblend* to the brush and fade the color to the right.

14 Dry the barn and use the detail brush to shadow the eaves with *Burnt Umber*. Blot the bottom edge of the eaves to create a glow.

15 Load the detail brush with *Burnt Sienna* and *Monoazo Orange* to paint thin lines separating the tin on the roof. Randomly add a few horizontal *Monoazo Orange* lines across a few of the roof sections. Smudge downward with *Clearblend*. Add a touch of watery *Burnt Umber* to the liner brush and paint the shadows in the barn doors, windows and plank details.

16 **Foreground:** Use your liner bush with a variety of watery grass colors to add a few tall grasses at the bottom of the canvas.

17 Tap some *sky blue* flowers on a few of the tall stems with a corner of the fan brush.

18 Clean your liner brush and load it with *Burnt Sienna*. Paint a small plow in front of the barn. Add a few sticks around the barn and throughout the meadow.

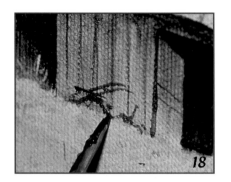

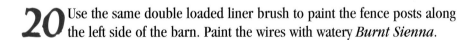

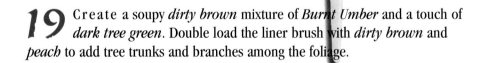

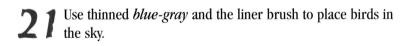

19 Create a soupy *dirty brown* mixture of *Burnt Umber* and a touch of *dark tree green*. Double load the liner brush with *dirty brown* and *peach* to add tree trunks and branches among the foliage.

20 Use the same double loaded liner brush to paint the fence posts along the left side of the barn. Paint the wires with watery *Burnt Sienna*.

21 Use thinned *blue-gray* and the liner brush to place birds in the sky.

Sign your painting and take a stroll "off the beaten path." Spray your thoroughly dry painting with Grumbacher Acrylic Painting Varnish.

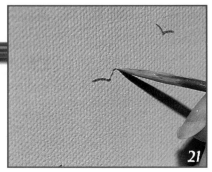

Grumbacher Artists' Acrylic Colors
Cadmium Yellow Medium
Cerulean Blue
Grumbacher Purple (Dioxazine Purple)
Grumbacher Gray
Hooker's Green
Monoazo Orange
Portrayt™
Thio™ Violet (Quinacridone Magenta)
Titanium White
Yellow Ochre Light

Brushes
2" gesso brush
Golden Edge™ #8 filbert brush
Golden Edge™ #2 liner brush
Gainsborough® #6 flat bristle brush
size 1 Bristle Fan brush
Sable Essence™ ½" angle brush
2" hake brush

Other Supplies
16"x20" stretched canvas
Grumbacher Acrylic Retarder
Grumbacher Acrylic Painting Varnish
Clearblend
Whiteblend
tapered painting knife
masking tape
graphite paper, stylus

Palette
Before you begin, prepare these color mixtures.
pale yellow—Whiteblend, Yellow Ochre Light
off-white—Titanium White, touch of Cadmium Yellow
  Medium
light violet-gray—medium violet-gray, Whiteblend
medium violet-gray—3 parts Grumbacher Gray,
  1 part Grumbacher Purple, 1 part Whiteblend
dark purple—2 parts Grumbacher Gray, 1 part
  Grumbacher Purple
teal—3 parts Whiteblend, 1 part Cerulean Blue
bright pink—Whiteblend, touch of Thio™ Violet, touch of
  Monoazo Orange
dark green—2 parts Grumbacher Gray, 1 part Hooker's
  Green

Prepare these color mixtures as you need them.
flesh—Portrayt™, Whiteblend
medium brown—Portrayt™, Grumbacher Purple
light brown—flesh, off-white
hot pink—bright pink, Thio™ Violet, Monoazo Orange
medium pink— bright pink, off-white
dark brown—2 parts Portrayt™, 1 part Thio™ Violet

1 Transfer the design with the waterline 6½" and the dune 8½"
above the lower edge of the canvas. Think of light radiating from
the top right corner to guide you in highlighting and shading. **Background:** Start at the top right corner. Use a gesso brush to cover ⅔ of
the sky with mixed *Whiteblend* and *pale yellow*. Use the uncleaned brush to apply
bright pink randomly into the lower part of the wet paint, extending upward. Apply
dashes of *light violet-gray* in the center and lower areas, then paint the remaining
sky and water *light violet-gray*. Add *medium violet-gray* to the brush to shade the
top left corner. Blend with a clean, towel-dried gesso brush; use a clean dry hake
brush for final blending. Streak *light violet-gray* horizontally across the water and
medium violet-gray across the beach. Without cleaning the brush, apply *light violet-gray* to the hill top, *medium violet gray* to the center, and *dark purple* to the
bottom. With a clean, towel-dried gesso brush, crunch into the wet paint to blend
and texture.

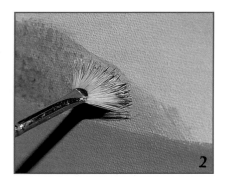

2 While the hill paint is still wet, use the fan brush with various brush-mixed values of green to add flecks to the hill, using lighter values near the top and darker ones as you move downward. Brush-mix *light violet-gray* with just a tiny touch of *dark green* and crunch in for the hill top; add *teal* to the brush and randomly add brighter touches. Add more *dark green* gradually as you work downward. Work quickly, and do not cover all the base color.

3 Load a clean gesso brush with *dark green* and a touch of *light violet-gray*, mixing it to a deeper green value. Crunch this in the center of the hill. Wipe excess paint onto a paper towel, add more *dark green* and crunch over the bottom section. Do not paint over all of the base color. Dry thoroughly.

4 Water: Brush *Clearblend* over the water and lower sky area; work these areas wet-on-wet, adding more *Clearblend* as needed to keep the areas workable. Use the angle brush to streak *teal* along the top edge of the horizon. With a fan brush, fade the color up into the *Clearblend*, leaving a distinct horizon line but no visible line as the *teal* disappears. Place a few streaks of *teal* and *medium pink* in the foreground water. Streak the beach with dashes of *bright pink*.

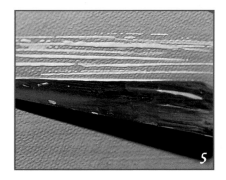

5 Starting at the horizon line, use the painting knife to apply *pale yellow* sparkles along the top center area of the distant water.

6 Create a gradual transition at each end of the highlighted area by brushing horizontally with the fan brush.

7 Lightly load the fan brush with *off-white* and add a few small breakers in the middle of the water area. Fade the bottoms and side edges with a clean filbert brush moistened with *Clearblend*. With a heavier load of *off-white* on the fan brush, crunch the crest of a larger wave below the middle breakers. Fade the bottom and side ends with a clean fan brush loaded with *teal* and *Clearblend*.

8 Load the painting knife with *off-white* and streak the tide line across the beach. Moisten the flat brush with *Clearblend* and brush horizontally to fade the tide line back into the water. Repeat, being careful not to disturb the previous tide line. Use various water colors on the liner brush to add tiny ripples to fill any voids.

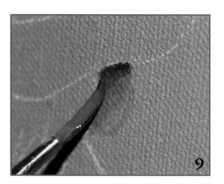

9 **Girl:** Transfer the girl, using charcoal graphite in the sky area and white graphite in the grassy area. Using the liner brush with *flesh,* paint her face and feet. While they are wet, shadow both with *medium brown*. Highlight the tops of her feet with *light brown*. Blend.

10 Apply and blend the basecoat colors for the girl's clothing a section at a time. Use the angle and filbert brushes. Following the lines of the pattern, shadow the folds of her dress with *light violet-gray*. Fill in the foremost fabric with *teal* and blend.

11 Base coat the back and derrière of the girl's dress with *teal*. For the remainder of her dress and book, alternate *teal* and *light violet-gray,* adding *Whiteblend* so you apply very pale *light violet-gray* and very pale *teal* in the foreground. Dry.

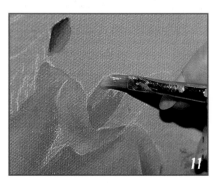

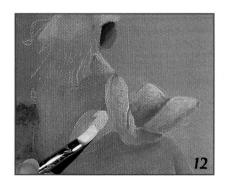

12 Highlight and blend one section of her book and clothing at a time, first covering them with acrylic retarder. Use the flat and liner brushes to apply the highlight colors, then blend with a *Clearblend*-moistened brush—be careful not to cover too much of the base color; check the highlights in the finished painting. Apply retarder, then *bright pink* and *pale yellow* to the top of the shoulder and sleeves; blend. Continue by applying *bright pink* along the shadow line under the arm, *pale yellow* on her bust, and the lightened *teal* from step 11 along her back. Use all three colors for the tops of her skirt folds and for her hat—lighten the hat colors and apply them more generously. Use the liner with watery *medium violet-gray* to add the fold and edge to the book. Dry.

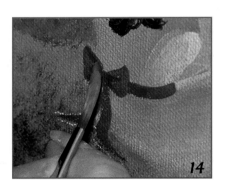

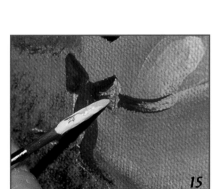

13 Beginning at the brim of her hat, base coat the girl's hair *dark brown*, using the angle brush to get a crisp line. Use a liner brush to pull down curls. Add a touch of *Grumbacher Gray* to the uncleaned brush and add streaks of shadow to the left side. Highlight a few streaks with *light brown*. Add *bright pink* to the uncleaned brush and highlight the right side.

14 Clean the liner brush and dry the canvas. Load the liner with *hot pink* and paint the sash around the girl's waist.

15 Add *Grumbacher Purple* to your uncleaned brush and shadow the sash. When the sash is dry, apply *medium pink* highlights. With the same brush, add a ribbon around her hat. Highlight the ribbon on her hat with *off-white*. Dry.

16 Reapply retarder to one section at a time in the areas to be highlighted. Blend the highlights as before. Add a touch of *off-white* to the top of the hat, shoulder, sleeve, chest, knee, ribbons, book and the center areas of water. Don't get carried away; too much will kill the glow. Dry. If touch-ups are needed, reapply the retarder before adding color.

17 **Grass:** Cover the area behind the girl with *Clearblend.* While it is wet, crunch *dark green* in the grass behind her to create a shadow; do not cover all the base color. Crunch a few *dark green* grasses beside her, overlapping the bottom edge of her dress. Blot the bottoms of the grasses to "plant" them.

18 Add the grass detail with *off-white* and varying values of *violet-gray, pink* and *pale yellow.* Use the fan brush to crunch lighter values at the top of the hill, medium values in the middle and dull colors in the shadow areas. Add more tube colors if needed. Add *dark green* to *light violet-gray* to accent the grass.

19 Use the gesso brush to crunch in larger, closer accents in the mid to low areas of the hill. Add *medium violet-gray* and *dark purple* to the uncleaned brush for the accents along the bottom and corners of the canvas.

20 Double load the liner brush with *medium violet-gray* and *pale yellow* to place a few birds flying in the sky.

Sign your painting with your favorite color, and go read a good book! To protect your thoroughly dry painting, spray with Grumbacher Acrylic Painting Varnish.

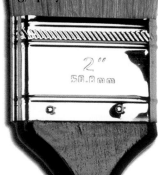

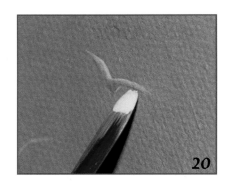

Large Mouth Bass

Grumbacher Artists' Acrylic Colors
Burnt Sienna
Burnt Umber
Hooker's Green
Iridescent White
Mars Black
Monoazo Orange
Thalo® Gold
Thio™ Violet
  (Quinacridone Magenta)
Ultramarine Blue
Yellow Ochre Light

Brushes
two 2" gesso brushes
#1 Bristle Fan brush
Sable Essence™ ½" angle brush
Golden Edge™ #2 liner brush
Golden Edge™ #8 filbert brush
hake brush
Golden Edge™ #6 flat detail brush
Multi-Texture brush

Other Supplies
16"x20" stretched canvas
Grumbacher Acrylic Painting Varnish
Clearblend
Whiteblend
Slowblend
natural sponge
tapered painting knife
masking tape
graphite paper, stylus

Palette
Before you begin, prepare these color mixtures.
cream—Whiteblend, touch of Yellow Ochre Light, touch of Slowblend
peach—Whiteblend, touch of Monoazo Orange
navy—6 parts Ultramarine Blue, 1 part Burnt Umber
blue-gray—navy, Whiteblend
yellow-green—2 parts Hooker's Green, 1 part Yellow Ochre Light
blue-green—Hooker's Green, navy

Prepare these color mixtures as you need them.
red—Thio™ Violet, Monoazo Orange, touch of navy
wheat—Whiteblend, Yellow Ochre Light
rusty gold—Monoazo Orange, Yellow Ochre Light
yellow—cream, Yellow Ochre

1 **Background:** Use a gesso brush to moisten your canvas with water; base coat with a mixture of *cream*. While the canvas is still wet, use the fan brush to randomly apply patches of *navy, blue-green, peach* and *yellow-green*. Concentrate most of the patches in the corners and at the bottom of the canvas. Blend quickly using a clean gesso brush with criss-cross strokes.

2 Using a clean hake brush, lightly blend the colors into a soft, blustery background. Dry. Transfer the pattern, placing the fish's eye 7" from the top of the canvas and 9½" from the left side.

(Note: It is better to paint the fish too light in value than too dark. After it is dry, it is much easier to darken it with a second wash of color than to lighten it. Should the fish become sticky while you are working, quickly dry it, cover it with *Clearblend* and resume painting wet into wet. This can be done as many times as needed.)

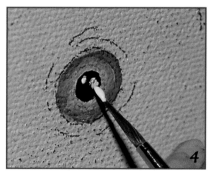

3 **Fish:** Use the filbert brush to apply *wheat* in the eye center and *rusty gold* around the outer edge. Blend slightly.

4 When the eye is completely dry, use the liner brush to add a black pupil in the center and dry. Place a *Whiteblend* catchlight at 1:00 and another at 9:00. Load a liner brush with watery *blue-green* and, following the lines of the pattern, add wrinkles around the eye.

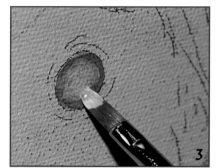

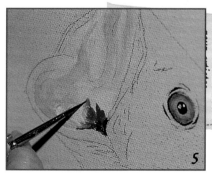

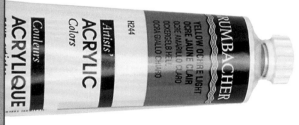

5 Use the angle brush to paint the mouth with a thin wash of *peach*. While it is wet, shadow it with *blue-gray* and blend the edges. With the liner brush, use dabs of *Thio*™ *Violet* and *red* to create a bright throat. Shadow around this area with *navy*. Dry.

6 Use the fan brush to apply *peach* halfway down from the end of the tail. Load the angle brush with *yellow-green* and streak it into the *peach*. Add *blue-green* to your brush and paint the remainder of the tail, slightly overlapping the *yellow-green*. With a clean Multi-Texture brush, slightly blend all three colors. Dry.

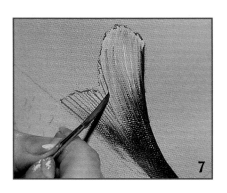

7 Load the liner brush with watery *blue-green* to paint the detail lines and a ragged outline around the tail tip. Use the same technique and colors to paint the dorsal (top) fin. Paint the bottom half of the fins along the back *blue-green*. While they're still wet, apply *peach* to the tips and use a clean Multi-Texture brush to blend slightly into the *blue-green*.

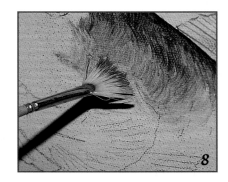

8 Cover the body with *Clearblend*. While it is still wet, apply *blue-green* alternating with *yellow-green* along the top of the back and head. Moisten the fan brush with *Clearblend* and blend these colors out into the wet *Clearblend*. Don't blend until the color is smooth and even, but rather make short, curved backward C-strokes to create a light-and-dark scaly effect. Tap around in the wet paint with a clean filbert brush to enhance the effect. End with a patchy color transition from *dark green* at the top of the fish to no color at the bottom. Dry thoroughly.

9 Again cover the body with *Clearblend*. Alternately apply *blue-green* and *yellow-green* along the bent area of the body. Add a few tiny dots of *Burnt Sienna* randomly into the greens. Blend as before from the bend toward the center of the fish, allowing the paint to become translucent and disappear before it reaches the gills.

10 While the body is wet, apply an irregular *blue-green* marking through the body center. Soften the edges of the stripe with a clean brush moistened with *Clearblend*.

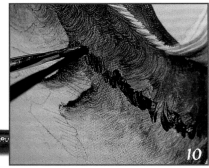

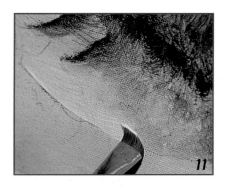

11

12

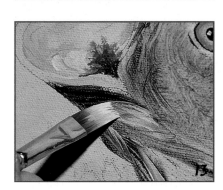

13

11 Use the angle brush with *peach* to paint the center bottom of the body. Paint *blue-gray* along the bottom of the bent portion. Blend upward, making it disappear just short of the *dark green*. Dry.

12 Cover the head, gills and most of the body with *Clearblend.* Follow the pattern lines to shadow under and around the gills with *blue-green*. Apply *blue-green* along the back and bottom of the gill cover (the disk-like area around and under the eye). While the gill cover is still wet, apply *peach* along the front and center. Pat-blend to create a scaly effect. Use the Multi-Texture brush with *peach* to paint the gills behind the gill cover, pectoral (side) and pelvic (bottom) fins; shadow them with *blue-gray*. Use the Multi-Texture brush to apply shadow streaks of *blue-green* for the gills under the head.

13 While the gill is still wet, load *peach* onto the Multi-Texture brush and apply it to the tips of the gills and fins, pulling it into the *blue-green* shadowed areas. To indicate scales along the side, use a liner brush with watery *blue-green* to make tiny staggered C-strokes.

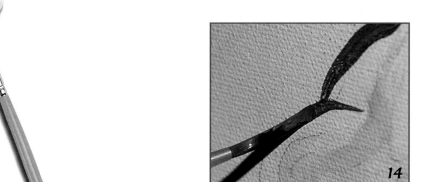

14

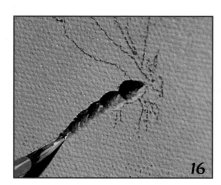

15

14 Use the liner with *blue-green* to paint the outer rim of the mouth. Highlight the top and bottom with *peach*. Fade the corners of the mouth with *blue-gray*. Dry.

15 Moisten the fish with *Clearblend*. Mix water and *Thalo® Gold;* apply randomly throughout the *dark green* areas of the fish. Blend the *Thalo® Gold* with your fan brush, leaving no hard edges. Apply *Clearblend* to the mouth, belly and fins. While these areas are still wet, cover with a wash of *Iridescent White*.

16 **Dragonfly:** With the liner brush, paint the top of the body *blue-green*. Dry, then paint his underside *yellow*.

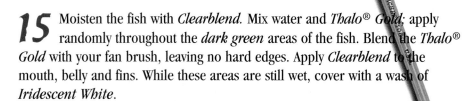

16

17 Use a detail brush to paint the wings *blue-gray* on the right and *Whiteblend* on the left side. Blend in the center.

18 After the dragonfly is completely dry, use the liner brush to do the detailing. Paint the head, legs and antennae watery *blue-green*. Use watery *blue-gray* to paint the markings on the wings.

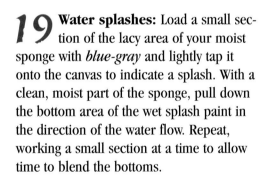

19 **Water splashes:** Load a small section of the lacy area of your moist sponge with *blue-gray* and lightly tap it onto the canvas to indicate a splash. With a clean, moist part of the sponge, pull down the bottom area of the wet splash paint in the direction of the water flow. Repeat, working a small section at a time to allow time to blend the bottoms.

20 Shield the fish with a piece of paper while you continue to create an erratic design of splashing water around him. After the blue-gray splashes are completely dried, use the same technique to apply splashes of *Whiteblend*. Place some Whiteblend splashes slightly above the top of the blue-gray, others in and around the water area. Blend the bottoms. With the liner brush and Whiteblend, add a few pronounced drops of water.

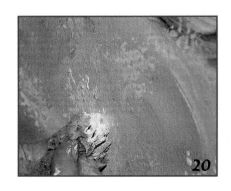

Sign your catch of the day! When it is thoroughly dry, spray with Grumbacher Acrylic Painting Varnish. Frame and go fishing!

Point Montera Light

Grumbacher Artists' Acrylic Colors
Burnt Umber
Hooker's Green
Mars Black
Monoazo Orange
Thalo® Green
Ultramarine Blue
Yellow Ochre Light

Brushes
2" gesso brush
#1 Bristle Fan brush
Sable Essence™ ½" angle brush
Golden Edge™ #6 flat detail brush
Golden Edge™ #2 liner brush
Professional™ #6 bristle filbert brush

Other Supplies
16"x20" stretched canvas
Grumbacher Acrylic Painting
  Varnish
Clearblend
Whiteblend
tapered painting knife
Rapidograph pen #.35
black India ink #3080F
natural sponge
T-square ruler
white charcoal pencil
masking tape
graphite paper, stylus

Palette
Before you begin, prepare these color mixtures.
sky blue—Whiteblend, Ultramarine Blue; touch of
  Burnt Umber
pale teal—1 part Whiteblend, 1 part Thalo® Green, 2
  parts Ultramarine Blue
pink—Whiteblend, Monoazo Orange
dark blue-green—2 parts Ultramarine Blue, 1 part
  Thalo® Green

Prepare these color mixtures as you need them.
charcoal—Ultramarine Blue, Burnt Umber
dark green—2 parts Hooker's Green, 1 part Burnt
  Umber
lavender-gray—Ultramarine Blue, Monoazo Orange,
  Whiteblend
tan—Burnt Umber, Whiteblend
cream—Whiteblend, touch of Yellow Ochre Light
rich brown—Burnt Umber, Monoazo Orange
  (marbleized)

1 Transfer the buildings to the canvas. Establish a horizon line with the T-square, then sketch the hill and road. Mark the walk platform, lighthouse bands, moldings and railings with the Rapidograph pen. To make sure they are properly aligned, hook the T-square to the side of the canvas. Cover the lighthouse with a design protector. Paint the ground and road *Mars Black*. Dry. Transfer the road with white graphite paper. **Sky:** Use a gesso brush with *Whiteblend* to cover the sky. Add *sky blue* to the brush and paint across the canvas top.

1

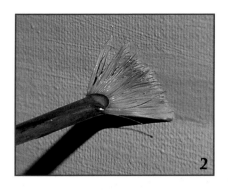

2 With a fan brush, randomly add streaks of *pale teal, sky blue* and *pink* throughout the sky so that the top section is darker. Blend slightly. Apply a streak of *pink* across the top of the horizon line. While the sky is still wet, use the fan brush to add *sky blue* cloud formations. Blend and dry.

3 Prepare your filbert brush for blending the cloud highlights by generously loading it with *Clearblend*, reshaping the brush and lightly wiping excess onto a paper towel. Load the corner of the fan brush with *Whiteblend*. Highlight and blend one cloud puff at a time: Dab *Whiteblend* on the top edge, then immediately pat with the filbert brush to blend the bottom and inner edges. Pat to blend the inner edge randomly, gradually moving into the cloud, until it disappears. Do not blend too smoothly. Create additional rolls on the clouds by skipping spaces between pats of the blending brush. Repeat, highlighting and blending as many times as you choose; rinse and reload the blending brush often.

4 **Distant Hills:** Use your angle brush with *sky blue* to paint the basic shape of the hills above the water line on the right side of the canvas. While they are still wet, add *pink* and *Whiteblend* highlights on the top and left sides of the hills. Add several highlight streaks throughout the hills. Blend the right sides of the highlights into the wet *sky blue*. Dry. Touch up, if needed, and use a brush loaded with *Clearblend* to gradually blend the edges of the wet touch-up paint over the hill.

5 **Water:** Use lighter values at the horizon, darker as you move downward. Use *sky blue* on the angle brush to paint the water below the horizon. Load the fan brush with *sky blue* to paint the center and foreground water, darkening by brush mixing in *Ultramarine Blue*. While the colors are wet, add streaks of *pale teal* throughout. Create ripples and blend slightly by using a "rocking chair" stroke with the fan brush. Use the painting knife or liner to place *Whiteblend* water lines along the horizon. To "plant" the water lines, randomly pat blend the bottoms and outer edges with a brush moistened with *Clearblend*.

6 Use the detail brush to place whitecaps in the middle water area; blend the bottom and outer edges as before. The whitecaps are smaller and closer together at the horizon line and become larger and farther apart in the foreground. Stagger the waves, painting them irregularly shaped and unevenly spaced.

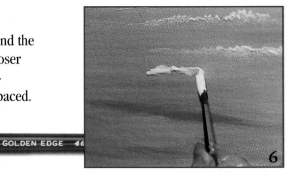

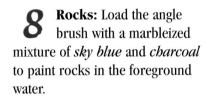

7 Load the fan brush with *Whiteblend* and crunch it into the foreground water to create whitecaps. Dry. Moisten a clean fan brush with *Clearblend* and blend the bottoms and edges.

8 **Rocks:** Load the angle brush with a marbleized mixture of *sky blue* and *charcoal* to paint rocks in the foreground water.

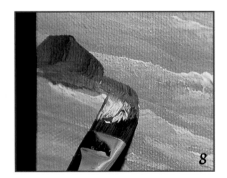

9 While the rocks are still wet, highlight the top of each with *pink* and *Whiteblend*. Add a small whitecap in front of each rock. Soften the bottoms of the whitecaps as in step 7. Dry.

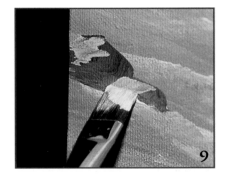

10 With a gesso brush, crunch in *dark green* grass on both sides of the road. Add *Yellow Ochre* and *Whiteblend* to the brush and highlight the grass. Crunch *sky blue* and *pale teal* highlights on the grass along the roadside and at the bottom of the canvas.

11 Apply *Clearblend* to the road with the fan and gesso brushes. While the road is wet, streak *Burnt Umber* across it. Add *pink* and *sky blue* highlights, keeping the strokes parallel with the canvas bottom. Blend slightly; dry.

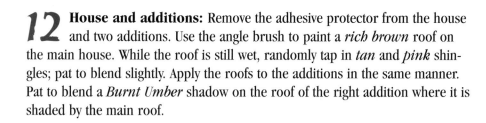

12 **House and additions:** Remove the adhesive protector from the house and two additions. Use the angle brush to paint a *rich brown* roof on the main house. While the roof is still wet, randomly tap in *tan* and *pink* shingles; pat to blend slightly. Apply the roofs to the additions in the same manner. Pat to blend a *Burnt Umber* shadow on the roof of the right addition where it is shaded by the main roof.

13 Use the angle brush to base coat the buildings *cream*. While they are wet, add *Burnt Umber* shadows and blend. Apply *sky blue* window panes to the right addition. Dry. Double load a liner brush with *charcoal* and *Whiteblend* to make the gutters and drain spouts. Dry. Use the liner brush loaded with watery *Burnt Umber* to detail the doors and window panes.

14 **Lighthouse:** Paint over the black markings; they will be visible through the paint. Retouch them after the paint is dry. Use the angle brush to paint the left side *cream* and to shadow the right side with *lavender-gray*. Overlap and blend the colors in the middle. Dry. Paint the roof *Monoazo Orange*; blend in a *Burnt Umber* shadow on the right. Fill in the top window and the portholes with *sky blue* and dry thoroughly. Use a liner loaded with watery *Mars Black* to paint the wrought iron railings and trim. Lay the canvas on a flat surface and darken the detail lines with the pen. Dry.

15 With the angle brush, tap in *lavender-gray* steps at the lighthouse base. Highlight with *Whiteblend*. Smudge with your finger. Use the liner brush with *Whiteblend* to highlight the bands around the lighthouse. Dry, then moisten the lighthouse with *Clearblend*. While it is still wet, apply rust stains randomly with *Monoazo Orange*. Fade the color down with a corner of the fan brush.

16 **Fence:** Refer to the finished painting for the placement of the fences along the roads. Sketch in a fence with a white charcoal pencil. Make the tallest fence post on the lighthouse side of the road 3½" tall and ⅜" wide. Sketch the tallest post on the right side about 2½" tall and ⅜" wide. As they approach the house, make each additional post shorter, smaller and closer to the last post.

17 Load the angle brush with *lavender-gray* to paint the larger foreground fence on the left side of the road. When the posts are dry, use the liner brush to highlight the left sides and tops with *Whiteblend*.

18 Paint the large fence on the right side of the canvas with *Whiteblend;* when it is dry, shade it with *lavender-gray*. Double load the liner brush with *lavender-gray* and *Whiteblend* to paint the short fences near the house.

19 Cover the road with *Clearblend*. While it is still wet, paint a watery *charcoal* fence shadow drifting across the road from the left fence.

20 Double load the liner brush with with *lavender-gray* and *Whiteblend* to paint the seagulls in the sky. With the liner brush and watery *Mars Black*, add a black tip at the end of each wing.

21 Load the fan brush with watery *Burnt Umber* and run your finger across the bristles to speckle the bottom of the road. Repeat successively with watery *dark blue-green, sky blue, pale teal, pink* and *charcoal*.

Sign and let your light shine. Spray your thoroughly dry painting with Grumbacher Acrylic Painting Varnish and enjoy!

Mementos

Grumbacher Artists' Acrylic Colors:
Burnt Umber
Iridescent White
Monoazo Orange
Thalo® Crimson
Thalo® Green
Titanium White
Ultramarine Blue
Yellow Ochre Light

Brushes:
two 2" gesso brushes
Gainsborough® #6 flat bristle brush
#1 Bristle Fan brush
Sable Essence™ ½" angle brush
Golden Edge™ #2 liner brush
2" hake brush

Other Supplies:
16"x20" stretched canvas
Grumbacher Acrylic Painting Varnish
Clearblend
Whiteblend
Grumbacher Modeling Paste
tapered painting knife
natural sponge
assorted ½"–2½" seashells
plastic fork
masking tape
graphite paper, stylus

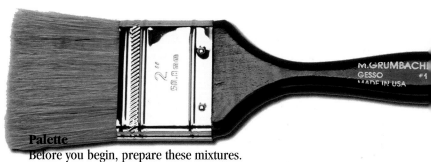

Palette
Before you begin, prepare these mixtures.
pale gray—1 part Whiteblend, 2 parts Ultramarine Blue, 1 part
   Burnt Umber
medium violet-gray—1 part Whiteblend, 3 parts Ultramarine Blue,
   2 parts Burnt Umber, 1 part Thalo® Crimson
marbleized peach—Whiteblend, Monoazo Orange

Prepare these color mixtures as you need them.
pale yellow—Whiteblend, Yellow Ochre Light
seafoam—1 part Whiteblend, 2 parts Thalo® Green, 1 part
   Ultramarine Blue
pale blue—Ultramarine Blue, Whiteblend
wheat—Whiteblend, Yellow Ochre Light
black—Ultramarine Blue, Burnt Umber, touch of Thalo® Crimson
off-white—Titanium White, touch of peach
dark gray—Whiteblend, Ultramarine Blue, Burnt Umber

1 **Canvas Preparation:** Transfer the pattern to the canvas so the water line is
6" above the lower edge of the canvas. Place the canvas on a flat surface and
use the painting knife to dab modeling paste into the water area, creating a rough
texture for the waves. Reload the knife and streak in the tide lines at a slight angle
below the water area, behind the dune. Apply a thick, irregular coat of modeling
paste onto the sand dune, tapering it across the bottom of the canvas.

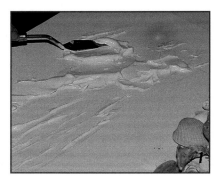

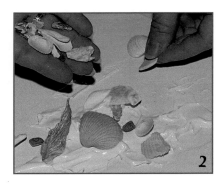

2 Firmly press a pleasant arrangement of seashells into the wet modeling paste.

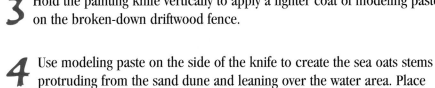

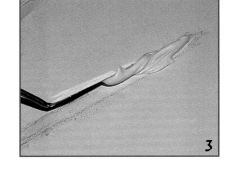

3 Hold the painting knife vertically to apply a lighter coat of modeling paste on the broken-down driftwood fence.

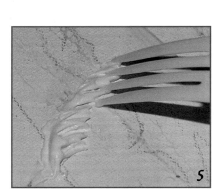

4 Use modeling paste on the side of the knife to create the sea oats stems protruding from the sand dune and leaning over the water area. Place modeling paste on the heads of the sea oats.

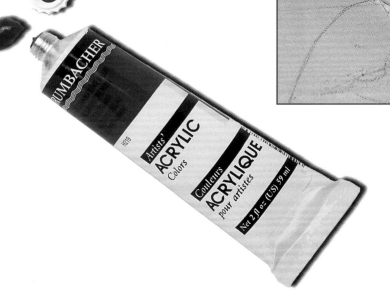

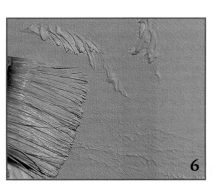

5 Create the illusion of separate seeds by lightly scraping the modeling paste on the sea oats heads with a plastic fork in a downward motion. Allow the canvas to dry overnight.

6 **Background:** Use a gesso brush with *pale gray* to cover the canvas, painting over the driftwood and sea oats. While it is wet, add a touch of *violet-gray* to your uncleaned brush and darken the corners of the canvas.

7 Continuing while the canvas is still wet, add more *violet-gray* to the uncleaned brush and scrub irregular cloud shadows in the sky. Blend with a clean, towel-dried gesso brush. Do the final blending with a clean, dry hake brush. Dry.

8 Apply *Clearblend* over the sky area with a clean gesso brush. Wipe the *Clearblend* out of the brush onto a paper towel. Lightly load a corner of the brush with *peach* and scumble highlights on top of and around in the cloud formations. While the highlights are still wet, add a touch of *Whiteblend* to the corner of the uncleaned brush and add a few brighter highlights.

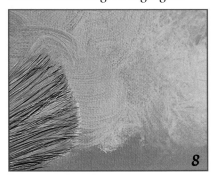

9 Fade out the edges with a clean gesso or fan brush moistened with *Clearblend*. Use the hake brush for final blending.

10 Use the fan brush to apply *Clearblend* across the bottom of the sky, touching the horizon. Brush mix *peach* and *Whiteblend* on the angle brush and apply it along the top of the horizon in the center of the canvas. While it is still wet, use a fan brush moistened with *Clearblend* to blend horizontally, gradually moving upward into the wet *Clearblend*. Create a gradual transition with a hard edge only where the sky meets the water.

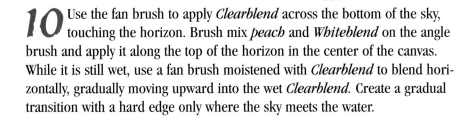

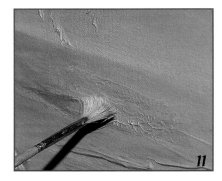

11 Cover the water area with *Clearblend*. Apply streaks of *seafoam* in the ocean area. Vary the shade occasionally by adding more *Thalo® Green* or *Ultramarine Blue* to the mixture. Dry.

12 Load the fan brush with *Whiteblend* and tap on white-caps. While they are wet, pull the bottom edges into elongated C-strokes. Apply the tide lines with the angle brush and *Whiteblend*. Use a clean fan brush moistened with *Clearblend* to blend the top edges of the wet tide line, brushing horizontally and moving gradually upward.

13 With the fan brush, add *violet-gray* shadows on the beach and under the tide lines. With the flat brush, dry brush *pale yellow, peach* and *off-white* highlights on the tops of the dunes. While the highlights are wet, soften the bottom edges of the paint with a clean fan brush moistened with *Clear-blend*. Apply *violet-gray* in the crevices over and between the seashells. Dry.

14 Get creative! Accent the shells with any colors you choose. Apply the accent colors with a **lightly** loaded fan or flat brush. To keep the colors vibrant and distinct, dry the shells and clean and dry your brush between colors. Add more tube color to some of the mixtures for exciting contrast. Don't be afraid to experiment—if you don't like a color, dry it and paint over it.

15 Load the fan brush with *pale yellow* to highlight more of the shells. Clean off the brush and continue highlighting the shells with *peach*. Strengthen the shadows in the crevices with *violet-gray*, varying the shadow colors by adding a hint more Thalo® Crimson or Ultramarine Blue to the mixture.

16 When the shells are dry, brush over the top ridges of a few shells with a thin coating of *Iridescent White*.

17 Use the sponge to tap a variety of colors—*peach, seafoam, violet-gray,* and *pale blue*—randomly on the foreground dune. Dry.

18 Load the angle brush with *dark gray* and paint the two textured fence-posts. Highlight the right sides with a combination of *Whiteblend, peach* and *pale yellow* to create reflected light. Add broken streaks of *seafoam* on the left sides of the posts. For the broken fishing lines blowing in the breeze, refer to the finished painting or transfer them again from the pattern. Paint them with the liner brush and watery *black*.

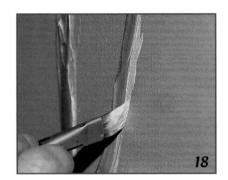

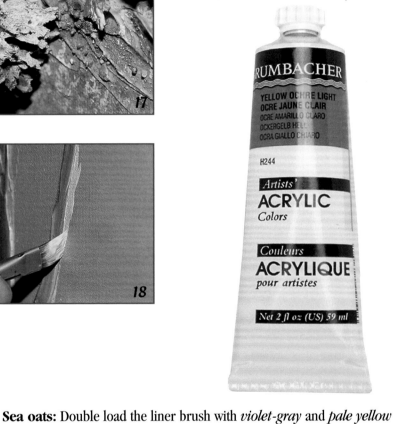

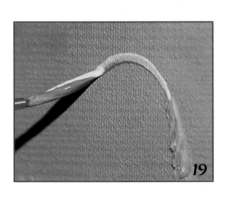

19 **Sea oats:** Double load the liner brush with *violet-gray* and *pale yellow* to paint the sea oat stems. Add some *peach* to the brush for the shadows.

20 Add a few more sea grasses at the base of the driftwood and along the beach. Use the fan brush to cover the tips of the sea oats with *wheat*.

21 Double load a liner brush with darkened *violet-gray* and *Whiteblend* to paint the gulls. Add the beaks with *pale yellow* and the wing tips with *black*.

Sign and treasure your mementos! When your painting is thoroughly dry, spray with Grumbacher Acrylic Painting Varnish.

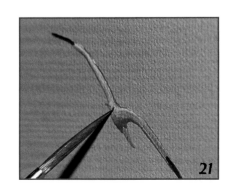

Coming Home, page 24

Evening Chores, page 42

Heritage, page 48

Large Mouth Bass, page 78

Mementos,
page 90

Nancy Drew, page 72

Off the Beaten Path, page 66

Point Montera Light, page 84

Remember When, page 36

Sergeant's
Reef,
page 18

Summer
Cottage,
page 60

Twilight Flight, page 30

Wanna Play?, page 54

96